Attitude 'Z'
Reign A to Z

Kathleen M. Luhrsen

To Erin
attitude 'z' Reign
Kathleen M. Luhrsen

Avid Readers Publishing Group
Lakewood, California

Attitude'Z' Reign A to Z

Copyright © 2013

by Kathleen M. Luhrsen

Avid Readers Publishing Group

http://www.avidreaderspg.com

Cover Art Kathleen M. Luhrsen

Book Graphics David Fabio

ISBN-13: 978-1-61286-164-7

Printed in the United States

CONTENTS

Chapter   **Page**

DEDICATION

To the wonder of my family and the blessings I receive from each one of them – I dedicate this book to ALL of you.

Dick, my husband and life partner; son Mike, and his wife Chrysa, and their son, Calvin; daughter Cindy, and her husband, Jeff, and their sons, Steven and Jim, and his wife, Angela, and their sons, Johnathan and Blake; son Randy, and his wife, Vicki; and daughter Rebecca, and her husband, Ed, and their daughters, Brenna, Ella, and Ava.

The circle of life continues..................

INTRODUCTION

Our *attitudes*,
anchored through our thoughts,
produce our behaviors and actions.

Starting this book, *Attitude 'Z' Reign A to Z,* has been agonizingly long; a struggle, a wrestling match, for I wanted it to be perfect. Moreover, even thinking about starting to write it, my mind produced thoughts of "What if? Who are you to think you can write anything on *attitudes*? Where are your credentials, Kathleen? Degrees?" In addition, I thought, "When I get a better *attitude* I'll be able to start the book." My inner dialogue did respond to that one saying, "Kathleen, maybe you will get a better *attitude* if you **start** writing the book." Thus, I decided my desire to delve into this *attitude* phenomenon was stronger than my doubts, and I was able and ready to begin this venture!

While on a much needed, but not thinking so at the time, week at the cabin with my husband for our 55th anniversary, I went to sit on the lagoon dock bench to, "just be." I had promised myself before that this place was reserved for being, gazing, and sitting - *no thinking!* Huh! That's nigh unto impossible! Even in meditation, one learns that thinking comes. That is what the mind does - think! Nevertheless, one can, through awareness and practice, expect thoughts, allow thoughts, know there will be thoughts, and then, let them flow through one's mind without trying to stop them or invite them to a resting place.

So, there I sat, observing the area, taking in the scents, and loving the view of nature: eagles soaring, fragrant pine trees, white lily pads and yellow locusts and I thought, "Oh this is perfect." But, then a tiny thought crept into my mind whispering, "Yes, but now if only a deer would come down to drink, the scene would be "more perfect.""

Fortunately, I continued musing that it had been perfect before and now I was adding something to make it a "new perfect." I realized, or did I become aware of, "When will it ever be ideal?" Do I have to add "something" to make it more perfect? Thus, the essay on "Perfect" jump-started this book, *Attitude 'Z' Reign A to Z* because I realized I was trying to make the scene more perfect instead of enjoying what I was seeing now.

As you journey down the path of reading this book on *attitudes*, you may find yourself stopping along the way to ponder an "aware" moment of how a particular thought has affected your behavior, action, and energy, which then affected the whole body, mind, and spirit. It is as if your "mind's eye" remembers and then hovers over a particular word or sentence. It stops your reading. So listen! Be "aware" that it is resonating with you, and perhaps you should give "it" time to process.

Therefore, allow yourself a moment to think and process your reaction. This book is not a marathon read. It may be a slow read, a life-changing read, or an awareness moment read. You might even ask yourself the question, "What do I think?" And, I am using this question at the end of each essay to reiterate that "what you think" is important and has consequences.

Deng Ming-Dao, in his book, *365 Tao Daily Meditations* says, "We speak and write to explain to ourselves." And this has certainly been true for me while writing this *Attitude 'Z'* book. I had to dig deep inside my own thinking to wonder, question, and ponder the "whys" of my *attitudes*, and many times, I had a "light bulb awareness" break through revelation. Thus, the "write to explain" that you can record on the "blackboard exercise" page in the back of the book, (as explained in the essay on "Thoughts") will open your "mind's door" to _____ [You can fill in the blank].

There are twenty-six extra blank pages in the back of this book for you to do your "thought writing" on whatever you feel inspired to note. That gives you a page for each letter essay. However, do not stop at the end of the page if something on your mind wants to keep flowing. Think outside your "programmed mind sheet per essay word" box!

You may have been subconsciously trying to get out of "box thinking" for sometime! Did you, as a child, before you entered school, color objects all over your drawing page? Then later in school, you were "conditioned" in an art class, for example, to put the sun in the upper one third of the paper; never on the lower right hand corner, as my daughter experienced in her 9th grade art class. In her imagination, she was inspired to draw the sun in the lower corner, but the teacher came by and said, "No, put the sun in the upper third of the page." Could she have been drawing a "setting sun?" So, think outside your programmed mind box when writing your thoughts or inspirations. Buy a notebook! You can then write to your heart's content. Options! Remember, we always have options!

This is a book on *attitudes*, and how many of them are formed by our just being on this planet. The above example, in an art class about sun placement, is a tiny reminder that *we do not have to stay within the twenty-six writing pages* with our daily life's thinking, for that immediately limits our expression. Is this a "thought seed" idea that we can use to evaluate other areas of our life on how we think? Are we becoming aware of, to be aware?

There is no right or wrong way to read this book, in fact, not reading it straight through from beginning to end is encouraged. If a certain word essay pops out at you and it is not sequential on the content page, listen, for your inner voice is, and it is trying to be heard. Remember the adage, "Life is a Journey, Not a Destination" also holds true when reading, *Attitude 'Z' Reign A to Z*.

Because this book on *attitudes* has taken up residence in my mind for at least ten years, I observed and pondered that our thoughts, and how we think, are an absolute in determining our behaviors and actions. Therefore, even though the "T" is in the 20th place in the English alphabet, I wrote on "Thoughts" next, for I believe they are critical in forming one's *attitude*. And, I was listening to **my** inner voice saying, "Kathleen, you do not have to be sequential!" (Sometimes I actually listen to my inspirations).

Therefore, I propose that, *Thoughts determine our day - our life!* I then follow my premise with: *The mind produces thoughts through our perception and conditioning (cultures, family, societies, experience to name a few), which form our attitudes on everything and therefore, determine our behaviors and actions.* Wow! The "Power of Thought," seems absolute! Moreover, if you will allow yourself to read the essay on "Thoughts" first, it will help you realize the importance that "your thoughts do affect your *attitudes.*"

There is an art to living life! Could the answer be in one's *attitudes*? Awareness, for living a well-crafted life, seems key to our doing it. In the book, *365 Tao Daily Meditations*, Deng Ming-Dao writes,

> The good of today is based on the good of yesterday. That is why we should constantly be attentive to our actions...

> Whether our lives are magnificent or wretched depends upon our ordering of daily details.

x

From that reading, I realized the same holds true for our own thoughts; so I injected the word, *thought,* for Deng Ming-Dao's words *good*, *actions*, and *details* to remind us of the power of our thinking. The saying then reads:

The [*thoughts*] of today [are] based on the [*thoughts*] of yesterday. That is why we should constantly be attentive to our [thoughts]…
Whether our lives are magnificent or wretched
depends upon our ordering of daily [*thoughts*].

When we become aware that *Today is Yesterday's Tomorrow* and our previous day's actions influence today's walk, we start to realize how critically important our thinking is to our day, our whole life. Yes! *The power of thought is absolute!*

As I was writing the book my plan was to stay with just one essay at a time, however, I found I could not do this. Ideas would overlap to another word, and actually become the word for another letter on which to write. Inspiration for the next essay was tied to the one I was working on. And, it dawned on me that this is what our *attitudes* for everything in our life are doing: they are intricately entwined in everything we do and say, and ultimately determine our behaviors. For example: our *attitudes* about a particular race may color all our actions on where we live, how we treat a clerk, what we might wear, how we treat one of our children's friends, to name a few. Hmm!

Because *attitude* is the key idea throughout all 26 essays, I am using the word, "Aware" for the letter "A." Until we become aware of something, how can we know how our *attitudes* are affecting our life? Awareness or awakening to something becomes like a blazing light shining through a keyhole-sized opening at the end of a deep dark tunnel to our mind, and we can finally see. Is being aware important to our *attitude* as I have been inferring in these "Introduction" pages? This will be explored further in the "Aware" essay.

For words that I have coined to emphasize certain thought images, I have included a "Glossary" at the end of this book for your further reference.

This is not a "how to book." It is an "awakening" book! It is "seed thoughts" planted, watered, and hoed by you, which will eventually blossom with the "awareness" fruit for you to harvest and nurture in your life. May it strengthen and enrich you today, and feed all your tomorrows.

Well! I did it! Trying to be perfect did not shut down my desire to write this book, for I firmly believe our *attitudes* influence our ability to live our life freely, joyously, and peacefully. Perhaps this is the true meaning of our life: to live life with joy, kindness, respect, serving, and love, so that we will make a "soft print" right where we are, wherever we are! This becomes our gift to future generations: We will have not been a negative life force; we will have been a "blessing." Our *attitudes* about ourselves, and how we view the world does determine our day and our life: *Attitude 'Z' Do Reign A to Z!*

What do **You** think?

P.S. I do know how to spell *attitudes*! When I was talking to my son, Randy, about the title for this book, he said, "Well, why don't you end the word *attitudes* with a 'Z' being that you're writing from A to Z words? Well I thought, "That would be fun and quirky; a different "play" on the word, thus, it became part of the title. Perhaps this is an example of how my thinking formed my *attitude* and determined my action. Hmm!

Chapter 1

AWARE

An *awakening* through
a "Keyhole Thought Vision"
to the mind.

The idea for the "Keyhole" *awareness* to our thinking was inspired by viewing a scene from nature on my trip up to Northern Minnesota.

I was riding in the car looking out the window at a grove of tall trees with gently bending branches when I saw a glimpse of the blue sky through a tiny opening. It was as if I was looking through a keyhole in a door to the other side. "Hmm," I thought, "This image is just like an opening to our mind when we become *aware* that how we think about something impacts our lives. This is a "keyhole thought vision moment!" It was an *awakening* moment for me, and the catalyst that stimulated this essay.

Our thoughts are our *mandala* (a pattern) for our life's path. To become mindful that our thought process is affecting this journey through our attitudes resulting in our behaviors and actions, is an awe-*awakening* moment; it is what I call a "Keyhole Thought Vision" moment. Is there power in being *aware*?

We might ask ourselves the question: Is this clear imaging of the "keyhole thoughts," a new phenomenon in the process of becoming "*aware* of being *aware,*" that our thoughts influence our life, thus our attitudes? Here is what Mary Margaret Funk, a Benedictine nun, has to say in her book, *Thoughts Matter*, "Early desert fathers and mothers of the third to fifth centuries noticed that thoughts and *awareness* of thoughts were the key to insight into the body, mind, and soul."(Italics mine) She also notes the mythical tale of Abba Anthony when "[he tells] about the vicissitudes of renouncing wealth, honor, status, relationships, and comfort only to find that the thoughts of wealth, honor, status, relationships, and comfort had followed him into his solitude."

Thus, Abbas (fathers) and Ammas (mothers) came to realize the importance of thought, and the impact their thinking was having in their life. They had literally gone to the desert alone to seek a deep, knowing, relationship with God and then, became *aware* that their "mind baggage" followed within them.

What they noticed in themselves eighteen hundred years ago we now call self-observation. Perhaps, it is even an *awakening* to us, that this idea of becoming *aware* is not new. Is anything really new or just a variation, a retooling of a previous idea in a new configuration? Isn't the world always looking to "build a better mousetrap?"

Each generation has to seek, find, and become *aware* of things for themselves. When we, as individuals, "see" for ourselves that our attitude is intricately tied to our thoughts, this realization will become "the key to insight into the body, mind, and soul" as Funk states above.

This *awareness*, this *awakening* of how our attitudes are affected by our thoughts, helps give us the power to do something about the way we think. Once we realize how we are thinking, we can change our thoughts and be empowered by the process. This act alone can still the agitated mind and bring inner peace as Lao Tzu wrote 2500 years ago, "To the mind that is still the whole universe surrenders. "

Lao Tzu's writing can be an "*awakening*" when we finally realize that to become *aware* is a moment of clarity, a moment of stillness. Usually that "moment" does not hit us on the head and say: "Well, now we are finally "*aware.* " Most of the time a "knowing," flows in like water seeping through a tiny crack, or like light shining through the keyhole. Knowing is a process of focusing or filtering thought. If we have been agitated, sad, hurt, depressed, or elated, happy, excited, (to name a few emotions and you can add yours), but have a moment of *awakening* or extreme clarity, it is because our soul, our very being, has been calling us to stop and notice what is going on.

Hopefully, we can "be still" long enough to recognize something is triggering a response, an *awareness*, of a particular emotion. Moreover, if we have been pondering how our attitude on a particular problem is affecting our very life through our behavior and actions, we can say, "I am *aware,* and I can change."

This may be a good time for you to write on the "blackboard exercise" page in the back of the book (explained in the essay on "Thoughts") of something that has been circling in your mind, and to now, finally address. Writing it down will give your musing a place to land! And, as Eckhart Tolle says in his book, *Stillness Speaks*: "With *awareness* comes transformation and freedom." (Italics mine)

Again, *aware*, is the *awareness* of being *aware*!

A very critical aspect of all this thinking about the importance for being *aware* of something, which is affecting our attitudes, our very life, is to be compassionate with our self. We must allow ourselves time to let this new observation "filter" into our mind. When we begin to look at a situation differently, the process of change has already begun simply by our recognizing the desire to change.

Sometimes, we will close the door on our *awareness* to a situation because we are not ready to accept it, and the *awakening* becomes "veiled" in our minds. Deng Ming - Dao writes in his book *365 Tao Daily Meditations*…"when knowledge threatens to show us our follies, we may realize that we are not yet ready to leave them behind. Then the veil closes again, and we sit meditating before it, trying to prepare ourselves for the moment when we dare to part the curtain completely."

Hopefully, that quote will give us the *awareness* and permission to not be too hard on our self, or to feel like we have failed in "working this insight." We must be very, very gentle with our self, as well as with other people! In fact, the quote from Mark 12:31(NASB) "You shall love your neighbor as yourself," says to me, "We need to love our self so we know how to love our neighbor." Could being kind to our self, first, help us be compassionate with other Homo sapiens, and then, extend that kindness to include all of creation?

Wow! When we start to "be *aware* of being *aware*", this process begins to transfer to everything we see, say, and do. The *awakening* through "Keyhole thought Vision" to our mind seems to lift the "veil" which has been covering our *awareness* that, "Attitude'Z' **do** Reign, A to Z" in our life!

Just a "Keyhole" thought for us to ponder in our "mind cave!"

What do **You** think?

Chapter 2

BELIEFS

Are they your *beliefs*
or someone else's?

Hmm! Take a minute, or as long as you need, to ponder the above question..............

What do you think? This reflection time can trigger many thoughts and we might ask questions such as "Does what and how I think come from my *beliefs?*" "Do my *beliefs*, which I think about and follow, form my attitudes which result in my actions and behaviors?"

Socrates (469-399 BC) said, "Life which is unexamined is not worth living." That's quite dramatic! This statement cuts to Socrates' core *belief* that it is imperative to use our own mind to decipher the myriad of ideas that have been thrust on us since we breathed our first breath and let out our first cry. That could be a long time ago!

Our *beliefs* on religion, politics, marriage, family, friends, work ethics, male/female roles, mother/father/sibling relationships, and all other *belief* possibilities, has been planted in our minds, either consciously or subconsciously, to form our "habitual thinking." As Wayne Dyer says in his book, *Excuses Begone*!: "I prefer to call this deeply programmed or almost automatic second-nature part of you, 'the habitual mind'."

Beliefs! Powerful? Behavior determining? Life driving? Yes! Yes! Yes!

So perhaps, if we are looking to alter or change our attitudes _____ (you fill in the blank,) we have to start "thinking" to flush out what, why, and how, we *believe.* We receive great inner power searching out the roots of our *beliefs.* We may discover our acceptance that something is true, has derived from someone else's *belief* system, and has then woven into our *beliefs* thinking. Take time to stop and think about this. Take the time to ask, "Does this *belief* system work for **me** in part or whole at this time?"

As a caveat, I must state here there is absolutely nothing wrong with our *beliefs* if they are what we truly *believe.* I only suggest that we open ourselves to **think** about our system of *beliefs.* Since many of them are programmed into us, I think it is good to stop periodically and ask our self, "Does it make sense? Does it fit, for me?" This may be the time to question, think about, journal, and finally, search out our own *tenets* about life. When it is our own *belief,* then it will flow peacefully and mesh with our whole body, mind, and spirit.

However, there is a caution about when we change an old thought pattern: we are so sure of our new *belief,* our new truth, that we want everyone else to *believe* as we do. Well, did not we just come out of that "thinking dungeon" originating from another's *belief* structure? Remember *belief* is personal! There is nothing wrong in sharing our beliefs. We just cannot force or insist that "our way" is the "only way" on other people; be it family, friends or the world!

6

Hmm, forcing *beliefs* on others! Hasn't this been the way of some Homo sapiens since the beginning of time? But, this can now be an awakening for where we are in our thinking, and we can decide to either accept or reject our previous learned *belief* system.

A good balance, at least for me, is to look to nature and watch animals. They eat, play, and rest. The parents take care of their young. They feed them, and teach them how to survive. When it is time for their offspring to leave their care and be on their own, they let them go. No musts, no have 'toos', no only ways, no parent's agendas to follow! I know nature is instinctual, but we, as human beings, have passed on a lot of "this is the only way" *belief* systems through human history.

It has happened through religion, politics, forced career paths, taking over family businesses and passing on *tenets* from one generation to the next, just to name a few. Again, someone else's *beliefs*, but are they yours? Try to remember the animals. Their young are sent off "to be who they are!"

Hopefully, all this reading and pondering the above "thought questions," are stimulating us to ask our self: "Are my attitudes, formed by my *belief* thoughts, influencing or determining my actions which affect my life working for me?" **Are they?** This might be a question to note on the blank pages in the back of this book. Using this "blackboard exercise" tool gives us permission to write what may have been stirring in our mind for some time about our *beliefs*. It might be a "key-hole" insight revelation to what **we** *believe!*

Our ideas change and we are still OK! We do not have to stay stuck in someone else's *beliefs.* Do you remember learning about Nicholas Copernicus' discovery that the earth was not flat? That new idea threw his known world into a dramatic turmoil because of the long held view that "the world was flat" and if you went to the edge, you would fall off. It was new information and resulted in a new way of thinking with endless possibilities for the people at that time in history and to future generations.

Copernicus lived from 1473 to 1543 AD. Here is a quote from his *DeRevolutionibus Oribium Coelestium* [1543]: "Finally, we shall place the Sun himself at the center of the Universe. All this is suggested by the systematic procession of events and the harmony of the whole Universe, if only we face the facts, as they say, 'with both eyes open.'"

I raise the above Copernican example to help us become aware that many of our convictions and *belief* systems are threaded through thousands of years of time. We still hold them ourselves because we have never stopped to examine if they still fit for us, personally, now. Mark Nepo in his book, *The Book of Awakening* says, "It seems we run our lives like trains speeding along a track laid down by others"

Therefore, my premise is that we step off the habitual track to explore our *belief* systems. This exploration opens a keyhole in our mind with new information and can help us examine our *beliefs* and perhaps, form new ones.

Remember, the incredible power to examine our *beliefs* and change them reside within each one of us. We just have to *remember*.

Easy to forget? Yes!
Hard to do? Oh, Yes!
Can You? **Yes! Yes! Yes!**

What do **You** think?

Chapter 3

CHANGE

Nothing *changes*.
Nothing *changes*!
Ernie Larson

Do you want to *change*? Are you aware of a need to *change?* Will the *change* alter your attitude, your behavior?

The thought of *change* can arouse high emotions to the extreme. We may ask our self, "Can I, do I, want to handle one more thing this ultraistic?" When we finally settle back from such emotionally charged thinking (see what power our thoughts have?) we realize that there are very few *changes* we can make or do to our life, which can be categorized as "extreme." What we can *change* is how we **think** about the prospect of *change*. Most people like stability, and it is our thoughts about the necessity of stability that have formed our attitudes toward *change*.

I would like to propose to you my thought of what I consider "extreme *change*" to be, in which all other alterations you might be considering for your life will pale in comparison. The most extreme *change* is – death.

Death is a *change* from which there is no return: death offers no chance to choose a different path. Remember, at least when you are living, your desire to alter something in your life can be done again, and again, and again - indefinitely.

With this example of *change* on the table, we can now keep our thinking about altering something in perspective. *Change* is not final! *Change*, is just a decision to do something a different way, knowing that if this adjustment does not work out, we can do it again. We are alive to *change* again.

However, when we begin to accept this new idea, that *change* is not final, it is still difficult to process in our mind that we are going to stop doing that "something" in our life. In reality, that "something" we are doing will end, but actually, "something" will also begin! Here are a few examples: quitting a job, you begin another; divorce, there will be another path, either being single or another relationship; moving across the country leaves the known, friends, restaurants, family, church, but new friends, restaurants and a church awaits your presence.

To give examples of *change* is difficult, for as many people are on this planet (over seven billion) is how many personal reasons there could be for *change*. Therefore, when offering ideas for *changes* in your life, I decided to draw a line like this _____
and let you fill in the blank for alterations you want to make. It then becomes your work, your thoughts, because only you have the knowledge and the awareness to decide if there is a need for an adjustment. In addition, if you can take a minute and transfer the filled in blank *change thought* to your "blackboard exercise" page in the back of this book, it will help keep you focused.

Yes, I know there are outside forces that can alter our life dramatically – forces over which we have no control, but even then, we still have the power within ourselves to choose to react and deal with them. Victor Frankl in his book *Man's Search For*

Meaning wrote about the positive power of choice when he realized he still had control over his thoughts. This happened when he was standing before his captors in a concentration camp, naked, with nowhere to put his hands. They had taken everything away from him: clothes, watch, ring, family, friends and his freedom, but he realized they could not take away how he was going to think about this situation. He wrote he was, "a being with a mind, with inner freedom, and personal value."

Our thinking "controls" our action (or inaction) to *alter* our lives, and that the power to *change* is always in the realm of our choice. Therefore, we must constantly remind our self that we have within us this ability to do "something" a different way.

This awareness and *changing* attitude is the key to how we view *change* and ultimately will give us the power and freedom to try! The thread of our thought determines our movements, and entwines through all we choose to do.

Change is scary! *Change* is exciting! *Change* is a new beginning. So, what are we waiting for? Waiting until all things are right? Waiting, for other people – whomever that may be, to decide our life? Waiting? Waiting? Waiting? But, if not now, **when?**

Albert Einstein said, "We cannot solve our problems with the same thinking we used when we created them." In other words, we keep thinking the same thoughts over, and over again, and somehow, we expect different results. This is habitual thinking, and using this rutted thinking, hinders our ability to *change*. Therefore, the awareness that "something" needs *changing* in our life is an insight triggered either by reading a book, an event, something somebody said or infinite other occurrences that slips through a "keyhole" into our mind and brings this new thought to the surface. And of course, when we awaken to this possibility we tend to want that *change* to happen, instantly!

Following is a poem I wrote on *"Change"* that appeared in my book, *Lord, Today I Choose to Live Life's Adventure.* I hope these thoughts will help lessen our self-imposed pressure to make everything happen – fast. This poem can remind us to begin, but it will take time:

CHANGE

Change takes
    new steps, little steps,
        big steps, monstrous steps.
They are taken
    one hour, one day,
        one week, one year.
They begin
    now, one second,
        one hour, one day.
But, *change* must start with me.

So, perhaps we need to remind ourselves again and again of what Mark Nepo says, "Our greatest chance to *change* our life is to close our habits of mind and to open our ever - virgin hearts. " (Italics mine)

What do **You** think?

Chapter 4

DOUBT

Are you allowing in your mind
the "*doubt* thread"
to weave into and strangle
your life's adventure?

Doubt versus self-confidence, are two attitudes, which compete against each other!

An instinctual "self-preservation attitude" in our mind helps keep the "*doubt* thread" from weaving into and entangling our self-perceived fragile self-image. Trying to keep *doubts* at bay can challenge our thinking one-step at a time over giant boulders of "What ifs? Who am I to try "this"? I am not smart enough, educated enough, or experienced enough!" My, how hard we are on ourselves! How we mentally beat up on ourselves! Yes, sometimes we are our own worst enemy!

We can not allow the mind to stroll down the *doubting* path for very long, because that negative attitude can lead to discouragement, frustration, and sadness to name a few of life's snuffing emotions. *Doubts* are strong thoughts! They will suck at our energy and bleed us dry of all hope, joy, creativity, and belief in our self. *Doubts* make it extremely hard to enforce the "Keep On Keeping On" motto in our thoughts, which is - perseverance.

Doubts are devious, insidious, demeaning, and subtle; especially when we allow them to grow in our mind. They can become an archenemy to our thinking pattern. If the "*doubt* thread" silently weaves through the fabric of our mind continually, it soon blocks off our enthusiasm, dreams, and passions with its tightly woven cloak.

Now remember, I am talking about negative *doubts*. Life snuffing *doubts! Doubting* our self, *doubts!* Being unsure can be a positive when we are questioning something; such as our job, a perceived answer to a science problem which doesn't seen to fit, a recipe that calls for one Tablespoon of salt to a one serving egg dish, and so on. Questioning something is a good thing when it helps us to search out an unsolved answer.

However, for this essay, we are working on developing an awareness of how our negative *doubts* can well up in our mind, control our life, and consequently, we cease living a "wonder filled" life. A *doubting* attitude becomes a ruse, a stratagem, a scheme to deceive ourselves from achieving our purpose that we feel consciously inspired to try. Therefore, we do not have the luxury of traveling very far along this negative thought path. The distance to turn around becomes longer with each uncertain *doubt* thought allowed. We must be vigilant and aware of the absolute power our thinking has in determining our life's journey.

"During the draft writing of these essays, it became enlightening to me that I did not write on "*doubt*" before this! For, *doubting* and debating myself during this writing process, wove a strong, thick thread through my mind, and of course, affected my attitude on particular days. I became aware of the power of *doubt* in my writing process.

14

I have considered many words for the letter "D" which could unfold the formation of our attitudes. Because I had so many choices, I was unsure of what subject to write about. I *doubted* my choices! Then, like a clunk on the head or a light shining through a keyhole into a dark room, I focused on the word "*Doubt.*" It finally became apparent to me, the word "*doubt,*" can be a negative "thought attitude" that really can "Reign A to Z."

If we wait too long in questioning ourselves, we start to feel unsure. For me, debating on this essay almost won! However, to renew my confidence I reread some of my previous essays to help release my "what if" fears. This action became a strong positive thread to help change my uncertain feelings, thus *Doubt* became the eighteenth essay I wrote.

We need to pay attention to where our thoughts are taking us and that we have the power to test and change our *doubts*. We can, with awareness and practice flip our *doubts* into self-confident thoughts.

Therefore, you might like to write on the "blackboard exercise" page in the back of this book any thoughts you are having about some of your "*doubts.*" The "Keep On Keeping On" motto might also be a good "perseverance" reminder to help keep you focused on self-confident thoughts. The scripture passage from James 1:6 (NASB) creates a graphic image about a *doubting* mind, and one that I often recall in my own "sea of *doubts.*" If it speaks to you, it can also be written down to help jog your memory; "But let [them] ask in faith without any *doubting*, for the one who *doubts* is like the surf of sea, driven and tossed by the wind." [Italic's mine]

While drafting this book, another tool I found useful in helping me deal with my own uncertainness, and especially helpful while writing these essays, was to write a contract with myself. It helps me when the "*doubt* thread" begins to enter my mind. I read it every morning to remind, reinforce and strengthen me to help stay with my inspired purpose to write on attitudes. It has kept me focused on my writing and is printed below, unedited:

I am committed to work and write
Attitude'Z' Reign A to Z.
I feel strong, focused, willing.
I will fit other chores and events
Into my writing day and time!
I can do this because God lives within me.
I know the power [able to be] resides within me.
God and I walk the same path.
All creation is good and I have
The Privilege - The Right – The Joy
to live in and through the wonderful
opportunity of it ALL.
I CAN NOT DO LESS!
I am so Blessed!
Thank you
Kathleen M Luhrsen
My contract with myself and God.

Could a contract with yourself help you with any of your *doubts*?

What do **You** think?

Chapter 5

ENCOURAGE

Encouragement, is an
"Uplifting life" seed
to an anxious receiver's
heart.

Consider the saying from the *Mother Goose Nursery Rhyme* "There was a little girl who had a little curl right in the middle of her forehead. When she was good, she was very, very good, and when she was bad she was horrid."

After deciding to write this essay on *Encourage*, that poem was a "Keyhole" awakening into my mind and I thought, "That is how we can feel and act in our daily life's journey. When we 'feel good' we are very good, and when we 'feel bad,' we feel horrible." How apropos was that idea to this essay message?

Both these good and bad feelings, which we allow to dwell within us, affect our attitude, resulting in our behavior and actions for the day, many days and maybe, years. Feeling good about what we are doing in our relationships, our job, etc., is communicated to the outside world, and, even more importantly, to our whole body, mind, and heart. When we feel discouraged, hurt, angry or any other possible negative emotion within ourselves, it mentally colors our day "dark grey gloom," and this attitude spreads out to all around us, and again, very importantly, to our whole being.

Then, someone gives us a word of *encouragement* gift. If we then take the time to receive it, believe it, think about it, and hold it in our minds, it becomes a treasure for that day. The word of *encouragement* can uplift our spirits and last us for many days to come. With this support, we climb out of our "dark mind pit" and start to believe in ourselves again, because the comment raises our spirits and helps change our mood.

Here is a wonderful quote from Proverbs 12:25 (NASB) that you might feel inspired to note on your "blackboard exercise" page; "Anxiety in the heart of a [person] weighs it down, but a good word makes it glad."

Because writing is such a solitary work and an author is so much in their own head, the challenge and danger is being stuck there. Feelings of doubt such as; "Why am I doing this?", "This is all junk!" can really hook onto our negative thought patterns, "coloring" our attitude about everything, and especially about our self. Our confidence can slip, and all these self-doubts can result in us lashing out at everyone and everything. No one around us can escape or is invulnerable, especially the people we love the most, our family. It is amazing how one word of *encouragement* can dispel the self-inflicted wound of doubt and all the other negative emotions that seem to crowd into our minds.

Remember, you do not have to be a writer to have discouragement happen. Anything that is happening in any person's life can cause this emotion, so you can write what you may feel discouraged about here _____ and it can be added to your "blackboard exercise" page to consider and write on further.

This *encouraging gift* was given to me the other morning when I was feeling discouraged, frustrated and unsure about the essays I have written so far. I was filled with doubt and gloom! Then my daughter stopped by to return some of the previous essay writings and give me her feedback. Now, this is my daughter, and one may expect that she will be kind, but she knows I want her gut reactions and her truth, so she proceeded to offer them to me.

She found the usual grammar errors, some unclear sentence structures, and misspelled words. But, her basic response to what I was trying to convey about each "word" essay was positive. She said she understood what I was trying to relate. She affirmed my premises, concepts, and reasoning and thought it even reinforced some of her thinking on the power of attitude awareness. She said the writings gave her mind, ideas to ponder (which is my main thrust for this book). She thought that people, through a new awareness about something they may be dealing with, would start to process for themselves about what, how, and if, they still agree and believe a particular idea. Unbeknownst to her, she *encouraged* me!

The marvelous wonder of that three-minute discussion lifted my spirits, and the grey gloomy clouds residing in my mind rolled away. Oh, the power of *encouraging* words! This event crystallized to me how the power of people's words, both positive and negative, can affect and influence our days!

That little encounter was the catalyst for this essay on *Encouragement*. I started to realize because of that brief talk with my daughter and her words of support, I was feeling better! *Encouraging* someone works, and affirming words do reinforce the Proverbs quote, "a good word makes [you feel] glad."

The message of this essay on *encouragement* is about bestowing positive affirmation to people. It also brings to light the awareness that negative comments can discourage and send people into further despair. Unfortunately, we are often totally unaware of the impact our words have on another person both positively and negatively. Now that we have been re-enlightened to the wonderful gift which *encouraging* words bring to someone we can process this premise, start to believe it, offer *encouragement* to other people and, probably the most difficult, and most important, accept it for ourselves. *Encouragement* fills us with courage to face ourselves! It is a "good thing."

Therefore, when an *encouraging word seed-gift* comes to you, plant it deep in your "mind soil" and let it grow. The fruit gathered (which is a better mood) at harvest time (which is every day's life encounters) will be rich and plentiful, and you will feel good! You will feel and be, very good!

Then, try giving the *encouragement gift* to someone else when the time presents itself. *Encouragement* raises the spirit of both the receiver and gifter, and helps each of you start to realize that, "Attitude does Reign!"

What do **You** think?

Chapter 6

FULFILLMENT

Ful - Fill Your Life.
You **are** - *"Ment"*
to be!

Wow! Truly accepting and believing you **are** *"ment"* to be, will color your attitude about everything you do on your life's journey!

Believing in "our self," frees us up to do the things that we feel deep in our soul. We can follow our inspirations, interests, dreams, and ambitions because we just "**are**" therefore, we can! But, do not forget the basic law of life: Not to harm or destroy other people traversing their life's purpose, while you are following your dreams!

Other people sometimes see the pursuit of *fulfilling* our ambitions as being selfish. However, remember these people have their own hurts, fears, family conditioning, and other personal inhibiting traits, which sends messages to their thoughts as reasons to suppress their inner drives. Therefore, they often transfer all those images of their un-*fulfillment* to you. (Do you remember back in the Belief essay where I wrote that people often try to force us to believe their way and be *fulfilled* as they are *fulfilled*? This doesn't work. We can never *fulfill* someone else's dreams for them.)

It is hard to be supportive to others while the person is battling their own thinking and attitudes of why they cannot do something. It is difficult to give encouragement to someone else's *fulfillment* when they are not able to do or follow their own ideas. In addition, either knowingly or unknowingly, they transfer that "virus" ("anything that corrupts or poisons the mind or character" *Webster's* definition) thinking to others.

But, believing and knowing we **are** *"ment"* to be allows us to break down those walls of outside influences or personal resistance and climb free to be; to be who we know we **are**!

Tough? Hard? Scary? Doubtful? Resistant? Oh, yes, yes, yes! But by following the deep inner voice that keeps calling us to listen and believe in our self, will and can rise to the top and let us do what we are *"ment"* to do. This premise is reinforced in Diane K Osbon's introduction to the book *A Joseph Campbell Companion* when she writes: "And, following your bliss, understood as Joseph meant it, is not self-indulgent, but vital: your whole physical system knows that this is the way to be alive in this world and the way to give to the world the very best that you have to offer." So, *fulfillment* is vital to our quality of life.

Because it is so hard to allow our dreams and ambitions in our self to come to fruition, it is imperative to feed our mind daily, as we do our bodies. Cars cannot run without gas or an electric charge and neither can our mind send out positive thoughts without being fed with positive input. Therefore, we should read our belief tradition's inspirational writings and teachings or self-help books everyday for our *fulfillment*. They remind us to work at believing in ourselves, and to act on that new awareness. They are designed to help each of us move toward personal *fulfillment*. And, the biography at the back of this book references a few books that will help us get started on our life *fulfillment* journey.

Our challenge is to keep believing and knowing that we **are** *"ment"* to be, and that it is OK to pursue our life's dreams. We **are** justified to do what it takes to reinforce this inner need and then, remembering this justification is only for our self! To other people, family, and friends, we just politely share our dreams. We do not have to rationalize anything to them!

Perhaps the hardest life decision to make is our need to *fulfill* our inner desires. We can always conjure up reasons and excuses to delay or deny our, "beginning - to begin"! But, it will help to remember a Confucius saying, "that a thousand mile journey begins with the first step." And the following is a good example with my own mind wrestling while writing this essay on, *Fulfillment.* I had read some of my morning devotions and other readings, and the word *"fulfill"* popped out at me. I wrote the word *fulfillment* down on a piece of paper and I saw three words: "ful - fill - ment" which I started to extend some meaning. They were **"*Ful*:"** I am all together. *"Fill:"* I can continue to fill myself up to live a satisfied life. *"Ment:"* I am "ment" to be here, so I can do what I need to do. It is OK." I pondered these ideas and thought, "maybe I should use *Fulfillment* for the letter 'F' essay." Then I fell into my habitual thinking (which I am working on to change) that, "I should get dressed first before I start to write. I need to sit at my desk. No, I should wait till I can write this essay without interruption. I need a big block of time; maybe go away to write." My inner critic was speaking too loud! And, that was just the tip of my "thinking" iceberg, to not begin writing, right now. My inner critic was discouraging me from starting!

It is hard for conditioned habits to die! I am a prime example! Then, something changed in my mind! I just sat myself down and started to write and write and write. Six pages later, I completed the first draft. I had taken the first step!

How apropos is this? I was *fulfilling* my desire to write on *fulfillment!* I am trying to learn that when inspiration hits stop, look, listen, and write! Then, either follow the inclination or "put it on the back burner." Just do something!

I hope this essay on *fulfillment,* is triggering a dream that is buried deep in your mind, which you want to bring into the "light." So, take a few minutes to let this "inner need" get used to the idea that it is finally being recognized through your thinking. Now quickly, without those thousands of negative voices or inner critics jumping in, write it down on the "blackboard exercise" page in the back of this book. This helps "your dawning awareness" of something important to see the light of day. Writing it down reinforces the power for that new awakening. It is another tool to use to help believe you can *fulfill* your desires for your life, because you **are** here! You **are** *"ment"* to be!

The joy, peace, and relief to our whole being will come when we finally recognize we truly **are** *"ment"* to be here on earth and that we have the privilege and the right to follow and *fulfill* our dreams. As Joseph Campbell says in the book, *A Joseph Campbell Companion* (selected and Edited by Diane K. Osbon,) "Follow your bliss," and, "A bit of advice given to a young Native American at the time of his initiation: 'As you go the way of life, you will see a great chasm. Jump. It is not as wide as you think.'"

You can be *fulfilled* because you **are** – *"ment"* to be!

What do **You** think?

Chapter 7

GRATEFUL

"Our world" looks softer
when we see it
through "*grateful* eyes!"

Serendipity strikes again!

I was walking up the stairs from the basement with a load of dried clothes after finishing a conversation with my husband, when I realized how lucky I was to be able to talk to him during the day. All of a sudden, I had this warm flow of thankfulness that we could still speak, see, and be together. I felt such a heartfelt rush of *gratefulness* and thought, "I now know what being *grateful* means."

I had been pondering what "letter-word" to write next and even though I had some word ideas, nothing was really speaking to me. Then I experienced that "a-ha" moment while having a simple conversation with my husband. It was a sensation of such pure joy just to be able to speak with him that I realized what unadulterated *gratefulness* was all about. And, I began to think, "Could "*grateful*" be my next "letter-word" on which to write?"

Serendipity moments do strike us unaware, and often stimulate the conscious thinking to process what has just happened. I began recognizing what feeling *grateful* was doing to my soul and how I was feeling peace within my body. Yet, when trying to put words to this reaction, I began to realize how inadequate I felt trying to describe this "eventful" moment. But, then I decided that if I defined *grateful* as "being thankful and appreciative of something or someone," that idea could be "seed thoughts" for our awareness. It could remind us of the impact a *grateful* attitude will have on our life and all those around us.

This book is a journey of how our attitudes affect our behaviors and actions by how we think. Therefore, pondering the word *grateful* and its meaning may add some softness, kindness and compassion both for our self, other people and our environment. The resulting attitude of *gratefulness* can thread itself through our self, our family, our jobs, our children, our friends, and even to our pets.

This could be a time or moment for you to write something you knowingly feel *grateful* for on the "blackboard exercise" page. The pondering and noting of your thinking may even stimulate your mind to other things (people etc.) that up to now, you were not even aware of how thankful you are for their being in your life.

John Marks Templeton in his book *Discovering the Laws of Life* says, "It is a law of life, and an inexorable [cannot be altered] principle, that if we develop an attitude of *gratitude*, our happiness will increase." (Italics mine) And, he goes on to say, "You may wonder how I can be so certain the law works. The only way to prove it to your self is to give it a good try and see what happens."

Well, it worked for me! Even if it was a serendipitous moment (the awakening to my feeling of *gratefulness* for being able to talk with my husband during the day) that revelation left me with a thanksgiving attitude. That feeling did thread itself through the rest of my day, and, hopefully, I will remember in the future. I do have to remind myself again, and again, that my life is a work in progress!

Being *grateful*, just feels good! It spreads through our body, mind, and spirit, and gives us a renewed sense of energy. It covers our inner being with a "golden glow beam," which we will reflect to our outer world. This is not a Pollyanna attitude, for it is, as Templeton said, "…if we develop an attitude of *gratitude* our happiness will increase." (Italics mine) As someone said, "Our face is the mirror of our soul," and when our soul is filled with *gratefulness* that cannot help but be seen in our countenance!

Therefore, we need to remember that it is our **awareness** of feeling *grateful,* which begins in and through ourselves, that is paramount to how we reflect that "attitude ray" to all we meet.

As in most things, until we realize that "if it is going to be, it is up to me," we will have to reflect, ponder, chew and digest this feeling of thankfulness for our self, to help continue this behavior. Then this "*grateful* attitude fabric" will cover all we meet, and its radiant beauty will remind us that:

"Our world" looks softer
when we see it
through "*grateful* eyes!"

What do **You** think?

Chapter 8

HAPPINESS

Happiness comes from within You!
If it has to come from anyone or anything else,
it can be taken away!

You control your own *happiness*! Oh boy! Here we go again! The responsibility for your life sits squarely on your shoulders with the realization that "If it is going to be, it is all up to me!" This means you, with all your fears and doubts! This wakeup call, as frightening as it is, can make you realize, "I am responsible for my own *happiness*." However, this awareness can also be a wonderful feeling of self-empowerment to know that "I **am** responsible for my own *happiness.*" You may even feel a gently flowing peace stream through your whole body, mind, and soul.

When we accept this fact, really accept this knowing, it finally takes the pressure off "them" and "things" to keep and make us *happy.* It is imperative to remember that if we allow or give over the power to control our *happiness* to anyone, then "they control our life, and they can take our perceived *happiness* 'need' away!" If we depend on someone or thing for our *happiness*, we are not free! We are captive to someone or something else. Being *happy* or unhappy is something we have to control for our own life.

The belief that, our *happiness* is totally dependent on something or someone outside our self, puts enormous stress on us by being "needy," and suffocating pressure on our friends, spouses, children, parents, or significant others to fulfill our desires. It is personally debilitating to "need" others to be responsible for our *happiness.* And, it is also a very heavy burden to have the sole responsibility for someone else's *happiness,* as some of us may well know, if we are the "giver" person.

If we perceive we are the "needy" or "giver" of *happiness,* it then takes joy and happiness away from living our own life's adventure. Both these behaviors are prisoners of habitual thinking. I hope we are starting to realize, that negative thoughts lead to negative attitudes, which cumulate in negative behaviors and actions. It just "ain't" healthy!

A revelation comes to these two behavior types when they finally realize and accept personally, that *Habit can change habit: I have the power within me to change a habit.* To form a habit we have to habitually think, act, and reinforce it over and over, and over, again. In the examples above, of a person being, either the "needer" or "giver" of *happiness,* the behavior has been continually aided by that individuals thinking. We even can reinforce each other's habits for being stuck in that groove. Our support seems stable and safe, but it is life draining – not life fulfilling.

Habit can change habit for a positive life action. If you are the "needy" type person, try planting the thought in your mind: *I am responsible for my happiness,* and then, repeat and reinforce that adage, again, and again, and again. I hope you will come to realize through the essays how the power of your "attitude thread" flows through and affects your whole life. If the above italicized "habit change" ideas speak to you, note them on your "blackboard exercise" page in the back of this book for later musings.

As the conditioned "giver," believing that you are responsible for another person's *happiness* is also a developed habit. Here, too, *Habit can change habit* with the realization that you have perpetuated the "giver" trap. Believing you are responsible for another's *happiness* snuffs out your joy and makes the "needy" person captive to you. You might also like to write down on your "blackboard exercise" page, *Habit can change habit,* and, *I am not responsible for another person's happiness.*

Hopefully, either the "needer or giver" of *happiness* is not using this as a "power tool" over the other person. We have to be very aware if we have developed this controlling behavior over someone.

Remember what you read in the essay "Change," where it stated, "Nothing Changes, Nothing Changes?" That maxim is a key to our awareness that we have to change how we view *happiness* if we are to alter our attitude and actions.

This awakening, that *happiness* comes from within and that no one or thing is responsible for your being *happy,* allows you to release, surrender, and let go of your conditioned habitual belief thinking; that *happiness* comes from outside yourself. The personal empowerment of this insight can birth encouragement in both the "needer" and "giver" of *happiness* freeing them up to live a "wonder filled," life adventure. They both now know that each person does control their own *happiness.*

Perhaps one of the best ways to keep a balance in our thinking is to spend some time out in nature. I know it is for me. While working on this essay an example literally flew up and landed in the big oak tree by my house. I was setting on the deck in a yellow wicker rocking chair drinking my first cup of coffee early in the morning and just "being." A gentle breeze was blowing the poplar tree's green leaves, and they all were dancing back and forth. I experienced peace, pure peace! Then a robin flew in, landed on an oak branch, and started singing. His notes were a song in the woods, and I thought, "He is just singing for no particular reason, as far as I know. Not to prove he can, not to gain anything, control anything, or because somebody say's he has too. He is just singing." Then I thought, "Maybe that is what being happy for a human being is. We just choose to work at being *happy*. I am not going to go into the scientific reasons why a bird sings, other then he does, and that we humans can be happy, because we can!

There are many examples in this world of people who have everything; money, fame, and infinite "toys," but are miserable, unhappy and always looking for that next "thing" which they think will make them *happier*. There are also instances of people who have very few world trappings. They do have food, clothing to protect their bodies, and simple shelter. Their health maybe fragile, but in the acceptance of what they have and how they live, they still choose to be *content*. There are volumes of intellectual analyses on these two different types of people of why they behave this way. Nevertheless, for here in this essay, it suffices for us to be aware that we do have a choice to be miserable or *happy* no matter what our circumstance. Miserable or *happy*? "It is your choice."

Nature can remind and restore, and the robin singing his song that morning was nature's way of restoring and refreshing my mind, body, and soul. I saw that to be *happy* is my choice, no matter what outside influences affects my life. Of course, knowing full well I **will** slip at times into unhappy thinking, the memory of that robin singing can remind me to "stay that *happiness* course."

As I said at the beginning of this essay, "*Happiness* comes from within you." The choice of how we view and pursue *happiness* is ours alone!

What do **You** think?

Chapter 9

INCLUSIVE

To have an *inclusive* attitude
towards people or groups is to believe
we are all part of the whole!

There are seven billion people in this world so that is a whole lot of "whole"! This tendency to be *inclusive* in our dealings with all of humanity is a challenge, and we have either been taught, "we are all part of the whole" through our family of origin or we have decided this for ourselves.

We need to become aware that if we label and then define ourselves, other people, ethnic groups, religions, or belief systems by how we identify them, we can create "locked in perception thinking" of that person or group of people. This thinking forms our attitudes and results in our behaviors and actions. Therefore, we need to be very aware of the impact and power that identifying and labeling people will have on our life, and all those we meet. This awareness can be a "keyhole" opening to our mind to remind us that, our attitudes do "Reign, A to Z!"

This essay is about the detriment to others and ourselves when we identify, label, and define a way of life, and then force, dictate, and suppress other people into bondage with our perceived attitude.

What rich life possibilities are lost when we start to "tag" ourselves by our jobs, our roles as mother, father, single, married, or senior citizen, for these labels can then become the substitute for our self-identification. The same wealth of opportunity to learn about other people is also lost when we designate and label our neighbors, our friends or strangers, and identify them exclusively with the mosque, church, synagogue, or temple down the street. Our labels limit people to two-dimensional cardboard cutouts of themselves!

We also lose the fantastic possibility of learning about, and from, the various cultures and ethnic groups. Could there be more similarity than dissimilarity with each other? If we do not identify, define, group, form and freeze our attitudes to support this "locked in" thinking, then we could discover our commonalities and learn from our differences.

As Deng Ming-Dao says in *365 Tao Daily Meditations*, "Identities only get in the way." Labeling one's self and other people has the possibility of limiting or stifling our own potential and the life of another person. Labels affect all the people we meet and deal with. Labels become our self-inflicted personal prison, and possibly, even literally, "locks in" any labeled person or group. Yes, as Ming-Dao continues to offer this sage advice "distinctions are superfluous" when this attitude works to exclude or consider other people or groups.

In my book, *Lord, Today I Choose to Live Life's Adventure,* I wrote, "There is always an open door to the world if I do not close my mind." I continued with the thought "Today, I release my 'locked in' thoughts and walk through to possibilities." As I reflect on those words of what would happen in my life if I close and isolate myself from an event or person, I found I would be living a very habitual thought life. No new idea would be allowed. No new view would be allowed. I too would have developed "locked in" perceptual thinking for my own life.

This restrictive thinking also happens outside our personal life when we exclude, label and define other cultures, religions, etc. We then have to protect, prove, or polarize these labels as truth that applies to everyone in a particular group. Wars have been started and fought because of this dogmatic, one way thinking!

Becoming *inclusive* in our thinking, we learn that with seven billion humans in this world, each person will see their world differently. We now can ask ourselves; Why should seven billion people ever have to live their time of life on this earth with the same perspective as everyone else? Why should seven billion people living in different geographical areas; deserts, oceans, mountains, have to live under one kind of thinking, determined by a few people?" Does this seem logical? Possible? Desirable? Should our world become one of colorless robots marching all in a line, mush for brains, staring dead eyed ahead? Sounds like this is from a page of a science fiction novel where someone is watching and controlling everything and everyone!

History reveals to us of times when absolute rule and one mind thinking prevailed, with sometimes devastating results. And, today's news shows us that excluding others, defining and grouping them, still is leading to horrific suppression. This information can help us think about the results an excluding attitude is having on humanity. When we finally decide all human beings are part of our universe, we form an *inclusive* attitude, and start to see people through softer, kinder eyes.

Maybe this is a good time for you to go to your "blackboard exercise" page and write down any "a-ha" thoughts you might have for identifying, labeling or defining friends, family, strangers, cultures etc. which this essay may have triggered in your mind. You may also want to ask the question: Is my "locked in" thinking detrimental to my personal growth to living a rich full life, and sharing and receiving the wonders of other people and their life? Could forming an *inclusive* attitude soften my view of the world to not exclude certain people? Then, take some time to reflect on this quote from Deng Ming-Dao about a muralist, setting a mosaic picture: "Every piece is precious. Together they make a priceless whole." This idea also refers to the human race!

I do not think this is a utopian way of thinking! I think it is a softer, kinder, more compassionate way to live our own life and bestow on others the right to do the same. It frees up our minds from focusing on conformity to exploring diversity. We are freer to embrace our differences and enjoy them. Dissimilarity expands our personhood.

I hope you decide to search and find the meaning and purpose in life that is yours, and to, intentionally live your created life without labels. As Joseph Campbell says in the book, *A Joseph Campbell Companion*, "Follow your bliss." Living your bliss is not allowed when we fall victim to and accept an, absolute thinking premise, that all people should follow one line of thinking, which can happen when we identify, then label, any person or group.

Can this "keyhole" awareness help us choose to discard our need to identify and label people, free ourselves, and the world? Can un-locking our "need to define" thinking, affect and change our attitudes thus our behavior and actions? Can our decision to be *inclusive* in our thinking towards other people happen when we finally decide, "we are all part of the whole?"

What do **You** think?

Chapter 10

JUDGMENTAL

A critical, *judging* attitude
does not
a kind behavior make!

Judging is all about defining something we perceive as correct or absolutely wrong. *Judging* people's behavior, cultures, religions, or politics, is dispensed through our thoughts from our conditioned learned habits. Therefore, it is helpful to step back, observe the potential results of our judgment calls and how they affect ourselves, someone else, or our environment around us.

We can see the results of *judgmental* condemnation throughout history. For example; Hitler's concentration camps for Jewish people and anyone who disagreed with him; or the ongoing practices for ethnic cleansing in today's world. *Judgment* can become a deadly poison: one that we should be aware of when we proceed to *judge* anything.

We have to be vigilant of what our thoughts can do in forming our attitudes for it shapes the actions we take. Just that trickle of awareness can help us to start thinking: "Is what I am saying or making distinctions about hurting or helping someone and/or myself."

Of course, here we meet the real challenge, the real call about being *judgmental*. Is it ever right to pronounce *judgment* on anything? Do we ever need to *judge* something that seems so morally wrong and evil to society as a whole and to people individually? Is there anyone, anywhere that has the right to "pronounce *judgment*?"

Here is the definition for *judgmental*, which gives us a basis or foundation for thought in this essay: "Making or tending to make *judgments* as to value, importance, etc., often specific, *judgment* considered to be lacking in tolerance, compassion, objectivity, etc."(Italics mine) *Webster's New World College Dictionary, fourth edition.* The key that relates to this essay, about a *judgmental* attitude, is the last part of the sentence, "*judgment* considered to be lacking in tolerance, compassion, objectivity etc." to people and things.

The use of this definition as criteria for being critical of something or someone helps us put in perspective, and become aware of our real motives. Are we *judging* to help or define? Do we want someone to change for their benefit of health and welfare, or because they should change to our perceived "right way?" This definition helps to think and discern the real reason for being condemnatory of someone or something. Keeping this definition in mind is not always easy to do, especially when there is an onslaught of reprobative (to disapprove of strongly; condemn) attitudes toward something or someone; but at the very least this insight will allow us to think about what we are doing with our personal convictions.

Pronouncing *judgment* on something seems to be part of the human make up. Believe me, I *judge* very well! The following example happened while I was writing this essay. I was looking out my living room window and watching snowflakes slowly falling in the woods covering the tree branches and ground with pure white. I perceived it as quiet, peaceful and serene. I thought, "How can anybody not enjoy the winter scene?" It then dawned on me (probably because I was writing on being *judgmental*) what I had just thought. I was making a decision call for all other humans, "how could they not love what I was viewing?" In your face, Kathleen! I suddenly became aware of my *judgmental* attitude with this scene. I hope this little scenario will remind us that it is not only the "biggies;" race, religion, politics, sexual orientation, and on and on and on, that are the important evaluations of people; but the daily, seemingly insignificant, critical analyses we make about everyone and everything.

This might be a good time to go to the "blackboard exercise" page and note if you have a *judgmental* nature. (Don't worry we all do.) It might also help to write down, and, what possibly is the key to your awakening, discern if your thought is resulting in a "*judgment* considered to be lacking in tolerance, compassion, objectivity, etc." All you can do is decide if this *judgment* will have an impact on your life and others and is a "good thing" or if not good, that a change in **your** thinking would produce a more positive effect.

Just being aware of our preconceived ideas can become a catalyst for thinking about a *judgmental* attitude. Awareness is critical in recognizing if there is a need for change. Also, remember to use "tolerance, compassion and objectivity," when considering "*judgmental* attitudes" with people, things or ourselves.

I offer the following thought for you to consider, ponder, reflect, and see if it speaks to you: *I am the vessel that holds (and can choose to empty) the attitude for being judgmental. I choose to fill the space with understanding, thus cultivating in my "mind soil" a non-judgmental attitude!*

What do **You** think?

Chapter 11

KINDNESS

Kindness, must always
be our driver
when needing to be right.

Serendipity strikes again!

I usually get up in the morning around 6:00 or 6:30a.m., but on awakening this day, I turned over and fell back to sleep. The sun was already up and that usually helps pop me out of bed; but my other catapult is a mind that begins thinking before my feet hit the floor.

I woke up the second time with a dream still flowing around in my head, which I was recalling as I turned over and stretched. As I lay there remembering the scenario, it was about a director, casting a father part for a movie. She was relating what moral qualities the actor was to portray when dealing with anyone with whom the "father" met in his daily life dealings. These attributes were the ability to discipline wisely, to show fairness, to be *kind* and compassionate, yet retain the capacity to be angry over a particular event or situation.

As I lay there processing what I was remembering about the dream, I thought of Jesus being angry outside the temple where it had become a market place to sell various wares. It was suppose to be a place of worship. Jesus directed anger to the event, yet he showed *kindness* and compassion when dealing with people and their individual situations. The *kindness* word was now front and center in my thinking.

I had started this essay on *kindness* before, but it was not flowing, and I was laboring too hard in what I wanted to say. I know, from experience, that even though writing can be a struggle, it should be over a word choice or a sentence structure, not the entire essay! When writing is moving along smoothly, it just feels right. "This didn't feel right." So I quit! I put it aside knowing that at the right time I would go back to work on it. I think I was being *kind* to myself then, and now I feel inspired to start the essay again!

At this point, I think it will be helpful to know the definition of *kindness* is, "the state, quality, or habit of being *kind*, a *kind* act or *kindly* treatment," (italics mine) as defined in *Webster's* dictionary. *Kindness* is a distinguishing trait of love. Love is defined in *Webster* as "a feeling of goodwill toward other people." Therefore, we need to plant the "loving-*kindness* habit seed" in our thinking to help generate within us the qualities of gentleness, *kindness*, and generosity so that we are able to offer these behaviors to people or events we encounter.

Being *kind* to others can also awaken in us the realization that this behavior affects ourselves personally. I think one of the greatest benefits from *kindness* to other individuals is the recognition that, *we are being kind to ourselves when we cease our need to be right*. If this sentence speaks to you write it on your "blackboard exercise" page as a "memory gift" in your next situation for a "be *kind*," action.

To help process our awareness of the "need to be right" in our life, and if "being right" seems to precede *kindness* in our thinking, we might have to ask ourselves the following questions: Is it really important for me to be right? Do I have a need to be right? Do I have to prove to everyone that I am right? Is this need embedded deep in my "habitual thinking mind," forming my attitude that everyone must see me as, always right?

I do think we have to ask ourselves if our need to be right over shadows our act for *kindness*. This takes some introspective thinking and may take us sometime to discern. Ultimately, however, we must think about it if we want to let go of this "have to be right" nature. *Kindness* softens the interactions between relationships and brings gentleness to our whole being. Now that **is** being good to our self!

The book, *The Dalai Lama, A Policy of Kindness* has a chapter on "*Kindness* and Compassion," and begins with this sentence, "Whether one believes in religion or not, and whether one believes in rebirth or not, there isn't anyone who doesn't appreciate *kindness* and compassion."(Italics mine) I know this is true for me! Do you appreciate the act of *kindness* and compassion in your life?

As human beings, we all have basic needs such as food, shelter, and clothing. We also have inner emotions of fear, worry, frustrations, anger, love, joy, family and relationship concerns, etc. People strive to live their lives the best way they know how: Sometimes succeeding, sometimes not! Therefore, an act of *kindness* to a person can soften a moment in their day. As Mark Nepo says in his book, *The Book of Awakening*, "We help each other thrive when the checking in with each other comes from a list of inner *kindness:* How do you feel today? Do you need any affirmation? Clarity? Support? Understanding?"(Italics mine) That simple act of "checking in" can have a powerful impact on someone's whole being: mind, body and soul!

The awareness of *kindly* actions in our many life's dealings and the affect it has on us is a "good thing," but remember, being human we will not always do so. Nevertheless, *kindness* is a "great habit forming" attitude to keep working on and that is all we marvelous human creatures can do: Show up and try!

What do You think?

Chapter 12

LIFE

Why not
get both feet wet
in the river of *life*?
Jump in!

Our attitudes are formed by how we view *life*. And, of course, there are seven billion points of views! However, for this book we are basically concerned with one viewpoint: Your view. For within you is where your thoughts originate, which form your attitudes, and result in your behavior and actions.

The question on *life*, its meaning and how we should live it has been discussed, dissected, debated, deliberated, and defined since the beginning of the thinking, observing human. Throughout history and in each period, the dialogue about the meaning of *life* continued through the knowledge accumulated at that time.

Sages, both past and present, then and now, spent and spend, a lifetime searching and relating their possible found answers to the question of the meaning of *life*. Periods of history change, but the perennial "question" of the meaning of *life* continues to thread itself through each generation to ponder, discuss, and try to find an answer.

We cannot live out our *life* using other people's answers for *life's* meaning. It seems like the dark mystery of "What is the meaning of *Life*?" cracks open when some insight enters into our "mind cave" and we decide to search out the answer for our self. Usually, it is a very lonely, internal wrestling discussion! As I am writing these words, it may be presumptuous of me to write an essay on the meaning of *life*! I struggle regularly with this question for my own *life's* journey: Am I living a good *life*? Am I doing what I "should" be doing? Who is determining the "should?" Me? Someone else? This is just the surface of my thinking. My thoughts can go 20,000 leagues deep into my "mind sea" with questions for my purpose in *life*. However, my fears start to ease when I realize I am not unique in my wonderings. I am comforted because I know I am not alone in this journey.

I finally became aware that what I can bring to this *"Life"* question is that I can ask the question! And, by your reading this essay, it may re-awaken in you any thoughts that you are considering that will bring meaning to your *life*. Moreover, you do not have to ask and answer it for anyone else, not your spouse, children, parents, friends, co-workers, or significant other. Reading Joseph Campbell reinforced the value of asking the "question" for me when he was asked the question, "What is the meaning of *life*."(Italics mine) His response was, "There is no meaning. We bring meaning to it" as Diane Osborn wrote in her introduction to the book, *A Joseph Campbell Companion.*

There is miraculous power in the above realization that **we** bring meaning to our own *life*. **We** can determine and choose for our self what we want and need to do. I think the brightest, most blazing light to our "awakening mind" are the thoughts: *Life is **mine** to live!* No one else is in this body. No one else has my mind. No one else has my soul. No one else knows what I know! Therefore, it is only I, which can bring meaning to my *life*! The wonderful challenge and excitement comes when we finally realize that the answers are within us, and all we have to do is take the time to ask the "question" for our self.

Certainly, reading, talking and counseling can be a huge help in our deliberations about what to do in our *life*time. However, the messages of other people's "shoulds" for us lend weight to what we think we "ought" to be doing. We get confused! Our challenge is to sift through all these ideas, and sort out what other people might think is good for us, what we think is good for us, and then decide: is it good for me or them? Again, to decipher all this information is up to you alone. As a result, discernment needs time, solitude, and meditation.

I suppose all this self-examining can seem very egoistical or self-centered. Remember, this is your *life* to be lived through your dreams, desires, and passion. Yours! True joy and peace in your soul is attained when you know what you are doing, how you are going to live your *life*, and you are actually doing it! Then all the friends you have or married partner or significant other or job or where you will live geographically will fall into place. You will know because you have a sense of well-being and satisfaction, and it feels right!

I also know that most of us, in fact very few, can say or do: "I'm going off to find my *life's* purpose." Most of us have been on this "*living*" journey for sometime, but, at least consciously or sub-consciously, we never stop asking the question "What is my purpose in *Life*?" So, keep asking the question. Every phase of our *life* requires us to ask the meaning and purpose of our *life*. This question can be an oft-repeated *mantra* and will keep us centered and focused.

Change! If you have read this book from beginning to here, you have already read the essay on "Change," where the quote at the beginning by Ernie Larson reminds us that if "Nothing changes – Nothing changes!" This seems to say that if we do not do something with our *life* that we initiate, it will not happen. Of course, something will, and it behooves us to decide if it is going to be our self or something else working the change. Moreover, as we go through our stages in *life,* we come to realize change is what *life* is all about. Therefore, it looks like the question "what is my purpose in *life?*" will be asked again, and again. We are in periods of flux throughout our personal journey making this "question" valid and not a self-centered fixation.

"What is my purpose in *life?*" is a searching question and a challenge for every one of us. But, Socrates' idea that "*Life* which is unexamined is not worth living," (Italics mine) is a fantastic reminder to do all the above, anytime, anywhere, any age! If Socrates' adage speaks to you, it might find a place on your "blackboard exercise" page to help remind you, that it is OK to examine and reexamine your *life* through all its stages. We give our "permission and OK" to so many things each day, so it is exciting to finally become aware that we can give **ourselves** permission to take the time to evaluate our *life!* It is a decision worth making! It is in our own best interest!

Life is a journey of one. You can take along guests, but it ultimately resorts back to just one. This is what I came to realize while meditating one day. It is not morbid thinking. It is reality, and our acceptance of this fact frees us up to enjoy and be in awe of this fantastic, exciting, *life* adventure that we are trekking. Enthusiasm for our *life* is the thought I used for the title of my last book, a devotional/journal a person could write in for three years: *Lord, Today I Choose To Live Life's Adventure.*

Life! Oh, to understand it! But, more importantly to *Live* it! So:

> Why not
> get both feet wet
> in the river of *life*?
> Jump in!

What do **You** think?

Chapter 13

MOVEMENT

Movement,
begets
energy!

"When you wake up – get up, and when you get up – do something!"
And, that gnome (a wise pithy saying) was planted deep in my
memory the first time I read it on a picture board in the room of
a person I was visiting in an assisted living residence.   It seemed
ironic to me for her to have that saying placed in such a prominent
place, because she definitely needed help with her personal needs:
food was brought to her three times a day and other people cleaned
her room. The saying made me wonder: "What did she have to do
when she woke up?"

As I was pondering the saying and my question about her, I realized
the phrase fed and *moved* her mind and spirit, even though her
body was not able to "get up" by herself. Those words of wisdom
kept her alive mentally.   It kept her agile spiritually.   When she
woke up and read the verse, she entered her day with the idea, that
by just being alive, she could be interested and involved in that
day, where she was, and still be able to interact with all the people
who *moved* in and out of her room.

A "chosen" attitude! Somehow, she decided (and because she had
practiced staying physically and mentally active all her life) that

she was going to do what she could do with her day. She could be happy where she was with how she was, and be active! Certainly, her thinking influenced her attitude and propelled her behavior by this decision.

For the rest of us, we can take this phrase and plant a new awareness in our thinking that "*Movement* Begets Energy" whether physical or mental. But, we all know just to *move* ourselves physically, or mentally, it is sometimes hard to do. For many of our emotions, fear, anger, frustration, worry, apathy or acedia (weariness of the soul) can influence even the desire to do something. Yet, I have found that just getting up from the chair stimulates my body to action; doing some chore gets me focused and releases the dormant energy from within.

The following is a possible scenario of how *moving* can recharge your energy and your body. You come home from a full day's activity and you feel absolutely wiped out! All you want to do is sit, for you are zapped! Yet, you have a meeting to attend or you are supposed to go bowling or to a show. But you really feel like you cannot *move!* You almost feel sick! Then, because you are committed, you drag yourself up, change your clothes and set off for your event.

Later, all of a sudden you realize, "I am feeling great!" You're talking to people, and you're interested and excited about what you are doing. You think, "What happened to me? I dragged myself to this with no energy to go, and now I am not tired or apathetic. I'm actually enthused with what I am doing!" What is the reason for this change of attitude? Well, you *moved!* You stirred your body and it became recharged. You have re-energized yourself. Now, here I must note that for the technical, medical, or scientific reasons for this energy release, there are limitless resources you can go to that will help you understand why and how this energy flow happens. However, I will insert here Isaac Newton's first law of *motion*, which I loosely interpret as: an object in *motion* stays in motion and an object at rest stays at rest. This physical law applies to us emotionally as well. If we *move* our minds, our thoughts begin to flow. We have more energy to tackle our mental tasks.

I love how the visual image of the following verse from Proverbs 26:14-15 (NASB) mentally triggers a reaction within me to "get going, Kathleen!"

> Like the door turns on its hinges,
> So does the sluggard on his bed.
> The sluggard buries his hand in the dish;
> He is weary bringing it to his mouth again.

Kinda graphic, huh!

Of course, we all know there are times when we are just tired! We have to respect our bodies, know our bodies, and be very aware to listen to that inner voice saying, "Enough is enough!" We just have to be careful not to stay "stuck" there in – inaction.

Motion is so important to keeping the energy flowing in our whole being, even if we can only *move* the mind, as did my friend who lived in that assisted living residence. *Moving*, even when it can only be the mind, is helpful to keep enthusiasm streaming through our attitudes resulting in how we live our life. This might be a good time to write the following phrase in your "blackboard exercise" notebook: "When I wake up – get up. And when I get up – do something."

It will also help to plant the *"Movement Begets Energy"* maxim seed in the soil of your mind, to nurture and grow for a rich "life' harvest!

What do **You** think?

Chapter 14

NOW

Today,
is
Yesterday's Tomorrow!

If we do not live in the *now*, we start losing all our yesterdays by thinking – projecting ourselves into our tomorrows. Being in the *now* is where we must truly live, for that is where we are *now*, where we are living, where we are. As I wrote in my 365 daily devotion book, *Lord, Today I Choose To Live Life's Adventure*:

> Life's events will roll into one big blur
> unless I start living in the moment.
> Today, I will see, hear, touch, and taste
> the briefness of *now*.

When you are truly in the *now,* you smell the "smells," taste the "tastes," hear the "hears," touch the "touch," and see the "sees!" Is not that what living in the moment is all about; to really smell, taste, hear, touch, and see our world "*now*" throughout our life's journey?

So, when you are hugging your lover, wrap yourself in the hug. When you are eating a piece of French silk pie, savor each bite slowly. When you are watching a sunset, follow the changing magenta, azure blue, golden yellow colors as they intensify, and then slowly fade to whispering grey/white blues. Wow! *Now* **that** is "being in the moment!" Because of all those truly lived "then times," you will be able to recall those images when you need some quiet, mental inner room, moments. In other words, "Live your projected tomorrow's memories today. You cannot live them tomorrow for today!"

One thing I have learned, and actually still learning, is "To savor the moment" as in eating a piece of French silk pie. If I am always planning the next project, event or the myriad of other things that can occur or I can do, I miss the sweet taste of the *now.* Always living in "out there" never gives me the "present moment" time to savor.

How can we know the wonder of our life's journey, (which returns through our memories of past living) if we are always running, planning or hurrying to our next perceived "that" will be better? We can't! Living in the *now* gives us memories that we have truly lived!

Wayne Muller says in his forward for Mark Nepo's book, *The Book of Awakening,* "A life well lived is firmly planted in the sweet soil of moments...fall in love with such moments." Reflecting on his words, I realize one of life's secrets for me: *I will immerse myself where I am planted.*

Being in the moment is so important to our attitude for the whole spectrum of our life's journey. Always projecting our thoughts "out there" to or for something else creates restless, unsatisfied thinking, which affects our body, mind, and spirit, and ultimately, how we weave our attitude thread to everything around us.

While writing this essay, I have been searching for an aphorism example that will help plant and reinforce our awareness that we only live in the "present moment!" And, I found a reflection note that I had written a few days earlier, from a devotion and Bible passage in my previous book, *Lord, Today I Choose To Live Life's Adventure*. I was thinking about the fact that it is "so easy to preach love and so hard to practice it." I then wrote the following: "Help me THIS DAY LORD to just do, and be in and with the day. Boy, writing on being in the present – the now – Hope I learn and Lord I could use an example to help accomplish this for me and that I could pass on...Thank you." (The above reflection is unedited.)

While reading my notes, I realized that just that morning I had reread an essay in Mark Nepo's book, *The Book Of Awakening* which was answering my asked for example, both for this essay and that devotional reflection. He wrote, "....but wherever I cannot bring my entire being, I am not there," and I had made a note in the margin stating, "I am where my breath is."

Answers do come! It dawned on me, that the example I had prayed for earlier in my devotion and to reinforce the essay *Now*, I had already jotted down a while back on the margin page of Nepo's essay. Only when I decided to spend a couple hours gathering my notes, staying in the moment and rereading my material for the essay *Now*, did I find the thread thought: "being in the present – the *now*" and the example I had prayed for: "I am where my breath is."

If this phrase speaks to you, "I am where my breath is," add it to your "blackboard exercise" on the blank pages at the back of this book, and write it as many times as you feel necessary to plant it in your mind for awareness. This written reminder will reinforce your thinking for being and staying in the present, the *now*; this moment of your life.

We program our brain for both positive and negative, good and bad, and these *mantra* exercises can help groove the mind to use our new thinking in accomplishing what we want: Start up our awareness for the *Now Power.* And, begin to realize that **we** control our decision "to live in the moment!"

Perhaps, in a matter of time, more of our decision-making will be based on an awareness of where we are, what we are doing, and why we are doing it. As Anthony De Mello, a Jesuit priest stated in his book *Awareness:* "Truth is sighted suddenly, as a result of a certain attitude."

Yes, our attitudes are entwined with our senses, which give us information through our thoughts, which determine our behavior and actions at that time or in the future. Trying to live in the moment is another action to our life's learning process. We must also remember our life is a "work in progress," because we are always learning and developing throughout our whole lifetime. Awareness of the power of *now* allows us to ask the questions that De Mello continues to write in his book when he asks, "Why not concentrate on the *now* instead of hoping for better times in the future? Why not understand the *now* instead of forgetting it and hoping for the future?" (Italics mine)

I end this essay with a prayer I wrote recently to help me try to remember what I want to do and yet can slip so easily:

"Lord,
Help me live today
so that my tomorrows
will not be filled
with yesterday's regrets."

*Now **IS** Now!*

*What do **You** think?*

Chapter 15

ONENESS

To label, define and identify people or things
is the beginning for "separateness seed" thinking.
It does not plant *"oneness"* attitude thoughts.

What alienation we pursue when we negatively label, define, or identify our co-workers, different religious traditions, ethnic groups, neighbors, or any other possibilities in the universe, by tagging them with our perception of "absolute" judgmental thinking. This attitude can contribute to becoming xenophobic (a fear or hatred of strangers or foreigners or anything foreign or strange) in our relations to others and the world.

Wars are fought because of "separateness seed" thinking and if we really look at the mangled bodies from those encounters, we will see what alienation and xenophobia can do. These scenes graphically convey the importance for our understanding the meaning of *oneness* in the world when we hear the African word *Ubuntu*, which loosely translates: "My humanity is caught up, is inextricably bound up in yours." The greeting creates awareness in our recognizing the *oneness* of all human beings, and that we are connected. It reminds us that there can be unity in spirit, even though we are different or diversified in our thinking.

The negative effect of alienation thinking is reinforced in Mark Nepo's book *The Book Of Awakening*, where he writes, "...

everything that divides and separates removes us from what is sacred and so weakens our chance for Joy." In separateness thinking, we seem to see the world and its people as "them vs. me, instead of them *and* me!" We polarize, divide and alienate ourselves from any possibility of understanding other people when we refuse to recognize our inter-connectedness as humans.

When we become aware of the universal life thread woven through all humanity, we recognize and admit to the *oneness* we share in all things. It is then that we soften our minds to see others with compassion and kindness, instead of harshness or judgment. We become aware of ourselves in them! We are metaphorically walking in their shoes! We sense their pain and joys! We finally realize we are a world family! Yes, "No [one] is an island entire of itself, every [one] is a piece of the continent, a part of the main;" wrote John Donne (1572-1631.)

The same insight is also found in the Bible. In Colossians 3:12-14, (NASB) we are reminded of what we can do to help with our *oneness* attitude thoughts "...put on a heart of compassion, kindness, humility, gentleness, patience; bearing with one another, and forgiving each other... And beyond all these things put on love, which is the perfect bond of unity."

This *oneness* wisdom is not a secret! The idea has been told and retold for eons. Thinking humans have longed realized the importance of the mutual inner core all human beings share. I wonder why we fight it so! I know I work on this *oneness* principle still!

This may be a good time to go to your "blackboard exercise" page and write how you feel on this separateness/*oneness* thinking. How does separateness/*oneness* play out in your life? Does your thinking lean your attitude more toward separateness or *oneness*?

The benefit for your gaining insight to these questions is how change can come about if there is a need for one. You may also feel inclined to write the previous quotes (Nepo's, Donne, Colossians or *Ubuntu*) or allow yourself to be inspired to write your own *mantra*.

With seven billion people in the world, there are seven billion different ideas on how to view and treat other people. But, all we have to be aware of, and concerned about, is how *we* think and treat people! That is the only thing we can manage, control, and change. *Our thoughts are where change has its power!* It is in realizing "If it is going to be it is up to me." And it starts with the idea of a '*oneness* seed thought' planted in our mind, right where we stand, right where we live." Sound insignificant? Well remember, a forest begins with one seed! Believing and offering the *Ubuntu* greeting of "My humanity is caught up, is inextricably bound up in yours", will also spread to wherever our daily life's journey takes us.

What do **You** think?

Chapter 16

PERFECT

Demanding *perfection* is the burr
that keeps us hobbling along in life.

I have seen a limit to all perfection;....
Psalm 119:96 (NASB)

Perfect.
>What is *perfect*?
>Is anything *perfect*?
>Who says it is *perfect*?
>Why do we want *perfect*?
>Are we taught to be *perfect*?
>Have we become slaves to wanting *perfect*?

Is our attitude for being "*perfect*" found in the above questions and thousands more? Do we view, live, and rule our life by how we answer these questions? Are we even aware that it is our attitude about *perfection* that is influencing our life? Is the quest for *perfection* hindering our happiness in life?

While I was up in Northern Minnesota, all these ideas and questions about *perfect* were brought into my awareness when observing a peaceful, serene setting in nature. I had walked through the woods to the lagoon to sit on the grey, weathered dock bench and just "be." A quiet place, which allows my mind, body and spirit to relax, be quiet, and wash the tension from my soul. After sitting down, I took a long deep breath, and while slowly exhaling I began to notice the white lily pads and yellow lotus buds floating on the mirror like still water. Being early in the morning, the flower heads were tightly closed, but after a while, they slowly opened as the blazing sun light crept over them. A tiny bird flew low over the motionless water to catch its morning feeding of insects.

Across from where I sat, a dead pine tree laid flat, extending out into the water. I thought its usefulness was over for this world when that tiny bird landed on the tree's dry branch about 30 feet away from the shore. No, I was wrong, the pine still had a purpose; it allowed the bird to land, way out there, where it would have been impossible otherwise. Even though it was dead, the tree still gave sanctuary to that living creature.

Again, gazing across the lagoon to the opposite shoreline, I saw the mirrored reflection of thick green pinewoods and an azure blue sky with puffy, white, cotton-like clouds slowly floating by. If the scene were turned upside down, one would not know the true view because of the flawless reflected image. Now that is stillness!

Soaking up nature's majestic cathedral setting was easing me into contentment, and I thought, "*Perfect*! Just, *perfect*!" But, then another thought crept into my mind; "If only a deer, maybe a doe and her fawn, would stroll down to the water's edge on the other side of the lagoon for its morning drink, then the scene would be ideal. Then, my time here would be *perfect*."

All of sudden I realized what I was doing! I had just been looking at all of nature's beauty, letting it still my soul, and feeling this peace wash over me, when that tiny, "if only" thought stole into my mind. (And that is the right word, "stole," for it was stealing my joy of the moment, the Now!) I thought, "**No** Kathleen, this is *perfect.* Right now, this is complete. If a deer walked down to the lagoon's edge I would have a different scene, a *New Perfect.*"

This instance gave me the awareness of how to view and understand what *perfect* means to me: that wherever I am I can see it as ideal for that moment. I do not have to add, "if only that were here, they were here, I was there and then, it would be complete, kind of thinking!"

Perfect is always in the eye of the beholder. When we just let go of all our life's conditioning of what *perfect* is, we will start to live and enjoy each of our life's *perfect* moments. This will help us to know and realize that if something is added at another time, we just will have a *New Perfect.*

The questions at the beginning of this essay may have been answered here or not! They are just questions to help us become aware of how we view, and what we believe, about the meaning of *perfect* for our self. And, with that insight, will come an awakening to the fact that our behaviors and actions follow what we believe about *perfection.*

Sometimes all we can do is ask the question to stimulate our awareness of something. This time it is how we are interpreting the concept of *perfect* for ourselves. The answer may come to us when we become aware of what we are doing to ourselves, and others, both mentally and physically, in our trying to attain absolute *perfection.* What do we gain? What do we lose?

The answers can only come when we ponder the questions and search out our own answers again, and again. Therefore, let us take the questions from the beginning of this essay and make them personal:

What is *perfect*?
Is anything *perfect?*
Who says it is *perfect?*
Why do *I* want *perfect?*
Was *I* taught to be *perfect?*
Have *I* become a slave to wanting *perfect?*

At this point, you might like to jot your musings on the "blackboard exercise" page in the back of this book, to which by now, you may have a well-worn path. Your writings will help you become aware that the "*perfection* burr" snagged in your mind has been influencing how you view and live your life in wanting everything *perfect*! Just as important is what you ask, expect and demand, from all your relationships: family, friends, and co-workers for them to be *perfect*. Listening to and acknowledging the answers to these questions may result in a softer, gentler, more compassionate way of understanding this *perfectionism* attitude. For what you think, of and for yourself, does reflect on **all** you meet!

Are you tired of hobbling along in your "be *perfect*" attitude? Perhaps it is time to take a different view. Allow all the *New Perfects* to happen in your life! Letting go of trying to be absolutely *perfect* in everything takes the pressure off you and the "freedom door" can now swing open! Joy and Peace can flow into your whole being when you finally accept and enjoy each *perfect* moment as it is!

What do **You** think**?**

Chapter 17

QUIT

Sometimes we *quit*
too soon; or not!

A decision for our life journey about whether we should *quit* something: our job, relationships, smoking, overeating, drinking, moving to another place, going on a trip, or as many other reasons as there are people in this world (seven billion) is based on if we think we can or not! "If we think we can, we can. If we think we can't, we can't!" Our thinking precedes our attitudes and if we follow our thoughts of: "What if?" we often *quit* too soon. But, if our thinking follows the line of "What **can** I do?" we start to feed our attitude with little bites of possibilities. We then can ask ourselves the following questions: "Maybe there is a way. Who can I talk with to help me make it happen? There may be a way and I will find it. I am strong enough in my own thinking and I will not *quit* too soon."

Now we are using our minds to think, "I can!" Just that thought starts to give us enough encouragement to try, to believe in our self, trust our self, for we start to realize we have the power within to make something happen.

If we plant the two word seeds "I can" into our mind soil and let them start to grow, then we begin to feel the confidence and power that these "I can" words have as they root themselves in our mind, branch out our thinking, and become our "attitude leaves." We have a renewed energy as "I can" grows through our whole body. The "I can" life force also carries a sense of peace. Just the words "I can" will bring stillness to the soul, for our soul knows all along we can, we just have to believe it.

"I can" are words that kick out the negative words "I can't." For here, too, these two latter tiny "word seeds" can start to take root in our "mind soil" forming the "I can't" thought branch, and blossoms into our "attitude leaves." Negative thinking also stems out to our whole body. The "I can't" thought nullifies our energy, drains trust and belief in our self, and feeds our attitude to *quit*.

Actually, these two sets of words are opposites, worlds apart, eons apart! It is up to you, which set of words you will allow to take up residence in your mind. Remember, you always have a choice! This might be a good time to go to your "blackboard exercise" page in the back of this book and write down, "If I think I can, I can. If I think I can't, I can't." And possibly add, "Do I sometimes *quit* too soon?" You, and only you, can write and ponder these thoughts. Dialogue with close friends and family can give you input, however, it is you that has to believe in the adage "If I think I can, I can" or deliberate an answer to the question "Do I *quit* too soon?" for change to happen.

The other side of the issue of *quitting* too soon is knowing when to *quit* something. This is as challenging to learn as stopping too soon. We often vacillate a long time with these thoughts out of fear we will let ourselves down or we worry that other people will think we failed. And here again, friends and family do have a huge input, either verbally or non-verbally (whether we want it or not) when we are wrestling with our decision "to quite" something.

Here again, if we use the adage "If I think I can, I can" then this will strengthen our choice that, it is OK to know when to *quit*. Through the exercise of writing down our thoughts in the back of this book, we will be aware of a particular situation, which is not working for us, and that *quitting* is not giving up but a good reason to take another path.

Perhaps it is also important to remember that when we decide to *quit* something, we also can re-decide to start it up again. This is the wonder and the mystery of being human and the miracle is that we truly do *always have a choice.*

All this thinking and pondering may seem very selfish and self-centered. However, our attitude does branch out to all the people we live with or encounter each day, and is determined by where our thoughts are taking us. Believing and trusting in our self "leafs" out a softer, kinder countenance to all. As a result, everyone benefits when we know *when not to quit too soon* or when *it is OK to quit!*

Sometimes we *quit*
too soon; or not!

What do **You** think?

Chapter 18

RELEASE

In *Release,*
there is
peace.

Is there something going on in your life that if you could *release* it would then bring peace to your mind, body and soul?

I doubt that, of the seven billion people in the world, each one of us does not have "something" that we would like to change in our personal life. For we all have things that bring tension and uncertainty to our days. Remember, our thinking affects our attitudes resulting in our behavior and actions to everyone, everything, everywhere, as I have been writing about throughout this book.

Because letting go or surrendering that "something" is so personal, this essay on *Release* will only have meaning if you can apply it to **you:** to your specific need!

As you have done throughout this book so far and hopefully, will continue to do with the remaining essays, I invite you to go to your "blackboard exercise" notebook page and write down your "*release* need" idea. Remember change happens when you become aware of the desire to alter something in your life that is no longer working for you or if let go, could make your days better. Writing down your concern will help you get it out of the "dark mind cave" and into the "light" where you can now acknowledge what your *release* need is.

There is a wonderful quote from Eckhart Tolle in his book, *The Power of Now* that I have memorized, which helps me in my own *release* process; it is "Surrender does not transform what *is*, at least not directly. Surrender transforms *you*." Your beginning cognizance of something you would like to let go of is in itself the "awareness key" that can and will "transform" you.

There are so many how to, self-help, and inspirational books out there for you to read on personal development, but I think the one source, the most important source, and the totally forgotten source, is **You**! You hold within you the key, the only key, to what you need! Friends, family and coworkers can observe, be aware of, even know, that "something" you are holding on to should or would be helpful for you to *release*. However, you, and only you, have the power to relinquish "it" once you recognize "it," can identify "it," and accept and inwardly know "it!" Talk about the freedom, emancipation, and the liberation you can experience. Wow! "Let Freedom Ring" as Gretchen Peters wrote in her song.

Now, the thousands of "mind questions" for even considering the prospect of *releasing* "it," start to swirl in our head from that old habitual thinking we practice so well. These questions can run the gamut from; What if we can't do it? Is it going to be hard to do? Are we too emotionally tied to the situation? Then the idea that we actually **can** decide to *release*, surrender, and let go of something pops into our head and starts a renewed thinking in our minds. For as in all things, our behavior and action begins with our thoughts, where the possibility for change begins to take root.

The question "Can I do this?" and the thought "I can let go" is once again only for you to decide, for it truly is up to you! Just remember: *When you release, there is peace. When there is peace, you will start to feel tension slide away from your whole being.* Now, that **is** peace!

I am going to end this essay on *Release* with a poem I wrote a few years ago titled, "There Is Peace in Letting Go." You will see that I am one of those seven billion humans who struggle to work on yielding "it" regularly.

"There Is Peace In Letting Go"

Peace fills my very soul,
when I completely *release* and let go.
All tension slides away
as I finally find my way.

There is peace in letting go!

Come to me, Lord, this day,
I am actually on my way.
All my trials I give to You,
for I'm tired of moving on "cue.".

There **is** peace in letting go!

The search for this world's gold
is a never ending load.
Breathlessly running the endless trail
hoping that I never fail.

Yes, there is **peace** in letting go!

With my mind and body tense,
and relationships strained raw,

73

this world's view to always "do"
cannot lead my life to You.

There is peace **in letting go**!

So I am here this day,
to at long last find "**our** together" way.
Releasing my desire to control,
finally, I have a peace-filled soul.

> ***There*** *is peace in letting go.*
> *There **is peace** in letting go.*
> *There is peace **in letting go!***

Release! **Can** we realize "it?"
Yes!
Realize we **can** *release* "it."

What do **You** think?

Chapter 19

SOFT

Be *Soft,*
like cotton
with yourself!

Be *Soft!* Be gentle with yourself! For when your thoughts, resulting in your attitude and culminating in your behavior are not hard, your whole body *softens* and feels lighter.

For this essay, we will start with a hand's on exercise first. Hopefully, it will help us get our "touch sense" activated to how *soft* feels and we can then transfer that "cotton ball *soft*" awareness to how our own body, mind, and spirit responds to the word *soft.* And, perhaps this insight will help influence and affect a kinder attitude in all areas of our life.

Take a cotton ball (which I am doing now while writing this essay) and gently roll it around your fingers. Feel the cushiony *softness* and transfer that *soft* sensation to your mind and body. Potentially, this exercise will quiet, if only for second, any harsh feelings you may be experiencing about yourself or other people.

I often think and talk about being kinder, gentler, and less critical with myself and other people and the world. I do try, but the truth of the matter about being *softer* with others, is that I first have to "be *soft* with myself," for that is when I can start looking at everything else with "gentler eyes!"

There is a wonderful quote by Walt Kelly, which was used in a 1970 "Pogo" cartoon where he said, "We have met the enemy and he is us." This example reminds me again to awaken to the fact: all change begins with me, within myself! I sometimes **can** be my worst enemy!

Reflecting on that example, I offer a definition quoted from *Webster's Dictionary* on the synonym of *soft*: "soft, in this connotation, implies an absence or reduction of all that is harsh, rough, too tense, etc." Using this definition could help reduce our behavior for having a critical, judgmental, and unforgiving stance of our self and others. When we let go and relax our outlook on our life and the world, we benefit first in our thoughts, and second in our body, which can certainly affect our attitude with everyone we meet. When we become aware of our harsh judgments of our self and other people, we begin to recognize that human behavior is the result of being human!

Hmm! Awakening? Life changing? Ultimately, world changing? Could a *softening* within ourselves become, "attitude change, changing attitude?"

While drafting this essay on *soft*, what helped me to start transferring this awareness for being gentler with myself, was the daily reading of a contract I had written for me to stay on track while working on my book. It begins with "To fit chores and events into my writing time." (You can reread the entire contract in the essay on "Doubt") I read this promise every morning to help me stay focused, for it is so easy to let other events, phone calls, household chores, and "10,000 things" take precedence and pull me away from writing each day.

Signing a contract with myself to perform a certain way can become very stressful. I therefore decided to become *soft* with myself, to be compassionate with myself, when a day saw no writing. And, Don Miguel Ruiz in his book *The Four Agreements,* also provided me with an easing up approach to my writing through his Fourth Agreement statement: "Always Do Your Best. Your best is going to change from moment to moment; it will be different when you are healthy as opposed to sick. Under any circumstance, simply do your best, and you will avoid self-judgment, self-abuse, and regret." These words of wisdom give me the "cotton cushion" I need to stay *soft* with myself, and ultimately, with other people during this long, solitary, writing process.

The antonyms (opposite) of *soft;* are; *hard; rough.* Both our *soft* or hard attitudes can determine our actions and behaviors, which will affect our daily interaction with family members and the community at large. Inter-dependence means mutual dependence with each other. Thus, it helps us to remember that when we treat other people with a *soft* nature we are aware and supportive of their presence, their life, their very essence, and that we, as humans, are entwined together. *Namaste* (I celebrate the place in you where we are both one.) in action!

Wayne Dyer has a wonderful statement in his book, *Change Your Thoughts Change your Life* where he writes "Introduce a *soft,* (Italics mine) non-action style to your life", and continues with, "Practice the way of non-action, or performing without effort."

An image, which I often return to when reminding myself to "perform without effort," occurred when I stood by a quiet, gently flowing stream. It was meandering through downed tree trunks, in and out of fallen branches, and picking up leaves that floated on its surface. The water was not forcing its way; it was just working its way "without effort" to where it eventually would flow into a river. Therefore, if we use that gently meandering non-forcing stream image when dealing with our daily chores, projects at work, relating to people etc., we can start to flow, ease up, and have a gentler attitude for our life encounters.

I am also going to apply this example of a gently flowing stream, as a metaphor, for being *softer* in our attitudes on life, and compare it to the image of a rushing, turbulent, overflowing river, which can destroy everything in its path. The latter depicts what can happen when we stay unyielding in our life dealings. We can literally wipe things out!

So, we have a choice! Do we, in our life's dealings, want to be like a wild, raging river mowing down everything in its path, or do we want to choose and decide to be gentler, less ridged, more relaxed; the presence of a *softer* countenance emulating from our whole body to the world around us? Having a *softer* attitude allows our self and other people we are affecting, space, and the right to be who we are all meant to be.

I know, for me, the second choice will certainly ease and relax my body, mind, and spirit if I develop and practice a gentler nature, and that image reflecting from me, will flow to all I meet. Might this be a good time for you to go to the "blackboard exercise" page to write down your choice, raging or flowing countenance?

Being *soft* with your self might be the thread to use while weaving the fabric for your life. "Attitude'Z'" **do,** "Reign A to Z!"

What do **You** think?

Chapter 20

THOUGHTS

Your *Thoughts*
determine your Day!

Your life reflects your *thoughts!* Sound absolute? Determined? Profound? Yes! And through the centuries sages, writers, and various religious traditions have spoken, written, and preached about one's *thoughts*, one's thinking, in a variety of ways.

"What you think, you look; what you think, you do; what you think, you are," stated Dr. Forrest C. Shaklee Sr. in the booklet *Thoughtsmenship, 10 rules for Happiness and Contentment.* His reflections reinforce the premise, that at any particular moment: "Your *Thoughts* Determine Your Day."

People say there are two absolutes in life: Death and Taxes. I propose a third: "*Thoughts* determine our behavior and our life." This proposal is confirmed first of all in my own life and actions by realizing, that whatever I think, wherever I allow my *thoughts* to take me, it will decide my behavior and my actions at that time. And, this "proposed absolute" I have also observed and learned through watching other people, and the reading of both current authors and sages of the past.

In the book *Brain - The Complete Mind*, written for National Geographic by Michael S. Sweeney, he states, "...more than a century ago psychologist William James had a radical idea 'Thinking is for doing.' he wrote. In that one simple sentence, he packed a lot of information. He meant, first of all, that thinking about an action expands the likelihood of doing it..." Perhaps we need to be very aware of the power that our *thoughts* have in controlling our actions!

Waking one morning the genesis for writing on the word *thoughts* started to take root in my mind. I finally crawled out of bed to put the words on paper because I could not fall back to sleep. Then in the bathroom, where I keep a set of flip devotion cards, I read that morning's devotion: "The first hour of waking is the rudder that guides the whole day" by Henry W. Beether. Upon reading that I mused, "My first hour of *thoughts* can certainly affect my day!" For as the lake changes color by how it is reflecting light, my *thoughts* and actions result in what seeps in and colors my mind. *Thoughts* set in motion how I react to situations, people, and myself.

Was reading that devotional flip card serendipitous? Coincidence? Inspiration? Whatever I call it, it certainly set in motion my thinking process, and reinforced my desire to put pen to paper to begin this essay on *Thoughts*.

"Thinking comes!" One learns in practicing meditation, that *thoughts* will stream in even when we do not want them to. The challenge is what to do with them? Which ones do we "Hold", and which ones to "Fold"? as Don Schlitz wrote in the "Gambler" song.

So, let us ask ourselves, "Who or what are we choosing to mirror or reflect which then colors all our decisions and actions to set in motion our thinking process?" This is answered when we become aware, that what we put in our mind from reading, observing, experiencing, or from our conditioned thinking will influence our *thoughts* and our actions. It is what we fix our *thoughts* upon, becoming truth for us, which determine our reality, our attitude, and our day! And, the results of this thinking can be either positive or negative depending on our reasoning, our drawing of conclusions, that then, affects our life. But, we can "be transformed by the renewing of [our] mind," as stated in Roman's 12:2 (NASB) when we finally realize the power our thinking has in controlling all we do.

The following quote is from a booklet, *How to Have a Good Day Every Day* by Norman Vincent Peale, where he stated,

> Basically, we are what we think. Marcus Aurelius Antonius, Roman emperor and philosopher, said, 'The world in which we live is determined by our *thoughts*.' Ralph Waldo Emerson told us, 'A man is what he thinks about all day long.'
> How may we have the right kind of *thoughts*? The tenor of our *thoughts* is determined to considerable degree by the first *thoughts* of the morning. So, it is important to condition the mind for the day. (Italics mine)

Do we see the thread from the ancient and near past to the present of these thinking, aware people, who discovered the critical importance of how our *thoughts* affect, actually rule, our daily life and our future? Are we becoming more aware of how our *thoughts* affect our attitudes, resulting in how we behave and act?

I often call negative *thoughts*, "the Crazies," for they are sharp spear-like *thoughts* flying, piercing, and plunging into my mind. If I allow them to penetrate and stay, they can "bleed" a rough day. I realize I need to be aware of what I am doing and allowing in my mind. Moreover, that many of my ideas have seeped in through my past influences. One way I can stop the escalating barrage of this negative thinking (as quickly as I become aware of what I am allowing in my mind) is to repeat to myself "My *thoughts* determine my day." Therefore, I know "it is important to condition the mind for the day" as Peal states in his booklet. This reminder might also help you by repeating his quote, again and again. However, you must remember to be gentle with yourself, because, being human, there is a tendency to set very high expectations for yourself!

So perhaps you can do an exercise, taken from your childhood school days when you had to write on the blackboard ten (maybe a hundred) times a phrase your teacher wanted planted forever in your young mind. If you can, take time now to write on one of the extra pages in the back of this book titled "blackboard exercises" "My *Thoughts* Determine My Day" as many times you feel is right for you. Then memorize the phrase to recall it at your first awareness that a negative *thought,* "the crazies", might make your day go astray. You also, at the same time, might like to write and memorize the following: "My body and mind feels lighter when my *thoughts* are lighter."

We have to embed both of these phrases deeply in our mind so that they will instantly pop up when we start slipping into the old habit of negative thinking. For these negative *thoughts* will spiral up and destroy that moment, that event, that day, that year, our life, if we allow them to continue.

But, the realization that *we can actually allow and control our thoughts,* is the "awareness ray" that can beam into the "cave of our mind" and generate the power for our thinking.

We can choose what we will do with our thoughts, as King Solomon wrote in Ecclesiastes 7:25 (NASB)

I directed my mind to know, to investigate,
and to seek wisdom and an explanation,
and to know the evil of folly
and the foolishness of madness.

Our **"Attitudes,"** determined by our perception of reality, formed by our *Thoughts,* do **"Reign, A to Z!**

What do **You** think?

Chapter 21

UNDERSTAND

To *understand* is the
"mental garment" we slip on
when forming a particular attitude.

Oh, the struggle we go through when trying to slip *understanding* something on over our head! It can hang up on our ears, and get caught in our eyes, even our mouth needs to remember to stay closed!

All our senses are influenced when trying to *understand* "Why did they let me go at work? Why is my child so sullen? Why won't my spouse talk to me? Why did a relationship end?" And on and on and on! All these wonderings are so hard and really affect our attitude as we go through all of life's happenings.

So, again, we need to look at our thoughts to see if what we are telling ourselves is helping or hindering our *understanding* of something. With this awakening, we can work on how our thinking is affecting our attitude.

There are infinite examples to help illustrate our *understanding* a situation, and the following are a few of them. When trying to grasp the reason why someone lashed out at us verbally we might start to think, "They had a bad morning; or it stems from their childhood; or they have just lost a parent." Justifying their actions or giving them our benefit of the doubt can help us deal with their behavior. This trying to *understand* certainly may soften the anger or resentment that can so quickly boil up in our head coloring our attitude for the day "dark grey gloom."

This is awareness! And to help form our attitude (of *understanding*) is to realize that sometimes all we can do is to accept, let go, or surrender and let that "*understanding* mental garment" slip easily over our head and move on.

This is not easy to do, but we are working on forming attitudes that enhance, enrich, and excite us for our daily life's journey. We need to always remember we choose where our thoughts take us. Of course, that is, once we finally are aware **we** have that power within us! Now that is something we must **really** fathom!

As we work on *understanding* things affecting our life or the world around us, the other side of that coin is **our** desire to be *understood*. "Please *understand* me" can be a daily *mantra*, as we engage in all our daily life happenings. If this craving to be *understood* is strong, it affects our attitude. This expectation now becomes paramount in our thinking and we forget that who we are, and what resides in us, is only for us to *understand*.

On this side of the coin, we also have to slip on the "*understanding* garment" for ourselves. Again, we must observe our thoughts to become aware that this "to be *understood*" desire has now become a "need" in our thinking. And, we have perpetuated and reinforced this need by thinking it is critical that other people *understand* us. Is it? Is it important? Is it really important that other people always *understand* what we are doing? Perhaps the only important thing is what we know and *understand* about our self! Hmm! How often we forget the personal power we have to manage and track our thoughts, to follow them or let them slip away.

We now can give **ourselves** the "gift of encouragement," and "benefit of the doubt." Just these two can reinforce our attitude to release the importance we have placed on trying to be *understood*. This awakening is what will allow us to slip on the *understanding* "mental garment" for our self!

This essay is the accumulation of my thinking, writing and rewriting on the word *"understand."* I woke up one morning with the word on my mind. And, as I laid there in bed pondering what to write, I decided to follow the adage I wrote for the essay on "Movement;" "When you wake up, get up, and when you get up, do something." *I got up,* and six pages later, here is that "something," a reflection on *understanding!*

You may be thinking now, "Easy for you to say and write, but it is so hard to be *understanding* at times or to let go of my wanting to be *understood*." Well, remember your life is a work in progress, and all you can do is show up and try. At least this idea is "food for thought" and you decide when and if you want to sample it! Therefore, this may be a good time for you to note on your "blackboard exercise" page something that you want to *understand* about individuals and society or how you would like to be *understood*. You may also want to jot down how your perception of things is affecting your attitude.

"Oh, what peace we often forfeit," wrote Joseph Scriven in 1868, for his hymn, "What a Friend We Have in Jesus," and what physical energy we use up when trying to *understand* or be *understood*. Perhaps we may as fisher people often do, "catch and release" our wanting and needing to know if it is absolutely essential we *understand* all things or always have to be *understood*. This new acceptance could help to make **our** day "one for *understanding*" and soften our attitude for ourselves, and everything we encounter!

What do You think?

Chapter 22

VISION

Everyone see's
with a different eye *vision*
than ours!

The above statement can give insight into helping us understand that we all evaluate things, people, cultures, belief systems, politicians, family, siblings, *anything*, by assessing it through our own eyes! Even though we physically see the same thing, we process it differently.

Is it not amazing, that anything can be agreed upon or even comprehended when members of the human family so often do not "see" things the same way? But, oh how we want, how important it is to us, and how much physical and mental energy we dispense, trying to persuade other people to see things the way we do!

Is it the inner need for validation, control, or the desire to share something with another person, that makes agreement important to humans? I know I can get into quite a snit when I try to make someone see what I "see," and it just isn't happening. But, then I realize no one can possibly see things through **my** eye balls! How can they? They do not have my eyesight perception just as I do not have theirs. This "seeing" stuff is a two way street and I cannot get piqued (feeling slighted) just because they cannot understand my "viewing" story. It seems to me that it is critical to my awareness that I recognize the following premise: *that everyone does see their world differently than I do.* If I do not do this, I will live a life full of frustration, agitation and assertions!

The scripture from Matthew 7:5 (NASB) says, "...first take the log out of your own eye; and then you will see clearly enough to take the speck out of [anyone else's] eyes." And, serendipity struck again this morning when I read the above passage, and thought, "Wow, Lord, I have been thinking about how to proceed with this essay and could use some ideas, and then I read this passage. This is good!"

I realized that the "log" in my eye could be anything that another person is not viewing the same way I am. One example might be my loving nature and the quiet solitude of living in the woods. Some people relish the city lights, people talking, and the hum of cars and buses. And, of course, we then have our different "seeing" about politics, religions, ethnic groups, abortion and homosexuals. Yes, it truly is "amazing that we can agree on anything" when we all view things through our perception that is our reality!

All we can do is plant the "awareness seed" in our mind that everyone "sees" with a different eye *vision,* and then marvel, that this is a "good thing!" How boring it would be if everyone all stared like robots with one programmed view of this fantastic world! The above scripture passage can help to remind us of our possible judging nature, and plant the idea for a softer, kinder, more compassionate thinking quality into our mind for respecting each other's *vision.* Can't hurt! Can help!

How we view things impact and affect everything we do. Marcel Proust has a wonderful quote that I have seeded in my "mind soil" to help me remember that I should view life with less insistence: "The real voyage of discovery consists not in seeking new landscapes but in having new eyes." This quote reminds me, it is "I" who has to see with "new eyes, because other people will see things differently. It is my *vision* that is "cloudy" not theirs! And, "the real voyage of discovery" is when "I" realize and release the desire for someone to understand my way of seeing something.

I, therefore, invite you once more, if the time feels right for you, to go to the "blackboard exercise" page and write down any examples you are aware of where your "eye *vision*" seems to differ from other people, such as a co-worker, family member, neighbor, or significant other. Remember also, that you can do nothing about how others see things, especially when we bear in mind there are seven billion people seeing the world with their own *visions*!

All this introspection is for our enlightenment that everyone sees with a different eye *vision* than ours. It is to help us understand there are "billions" of views out there, and this awakening takes the pressure off us in determining for other people what they should be "seeing" or our feeling "piqued" if they do not! We can change our perceiving reality and our insisting behavior into one that realizes, **attitude** does "Reign A to Z."

What do **You** think?

Chapter 23

WATCH

> You and only you,
> are the "*watch*dog,"
> of your thoughts.

You are the "*watch*dog" of your thoughts! This awareness holds power for you as a human being. It reminds you that you can manage your own life by *watching* your thoughts, following them, or letting them slip away. Now that is self-empowerment! *Watching* what you think and then realizing how your thoughts affect every arena in your life is critical for attitude awareness.

For the letter "W" in this alphabet essay writing, I had been writing down various words that could help us be more aware of how our attitude influences everything we do, everyday. I had listed words such as wonder, wait, and willingness. Any one of them could have an impact on our attitudes. Then while reading a chapter in Mary Margaret Funk's book, *Thoughts Matter* the word "*watchfulness*" held my attention for a second. I continued to read the next few paragraphs, but my mind would not let go of the word *watchfulness*. I kept thinking about the word and going back to it. I finished the chapter, but that word was staying front and center in my mind. Then, I started to tie it in with attitudes, and realized how critically important it is for us to be *watchful* of how our attitudes affect everything. Because of this reading, I concluded *watch* was a very important "awareness" word that could help us in our daily life's journey. Therefore, "*Watchfulness* steps up the guard," (Italics mine) stated Funk in that chapter, when we finally become aware to *watch* over our own thinking.

There are many things we "*watch*dog" in our life: children, job projects, neighbor's fences, community, council, legislature, even our President. We follow that up, with our *watchfulness* of religious beliefs other than our own, different ethnic groups, and the world. That is a lot of *watching*! But, when and do we ever *watch* over our own thinking, which influences all our behavior interactions with other people, events, and ourselves? Therefore, guarding, reflecting, and pondering our thoughts are critical to what we will do with these ideas, and that where they are taking us is working for us, and us alone!

This, might be a good opportunity for you to write on the "blackboard exercise" page in the back of the book, some thoughts you would like to *watch* and guard over. Ideas can pop into our mind so quickly, that it is always good to acknowledge them immediately and then, ponder over later.

Perhaps you are now thinking, "Oh my, one more thing I have to observe, to be vigilant in doing, one more thing!" But, **you** are important! It is more important to be aware of where your thoughts are taking you, which are forming all your attitudes about life, than being involved in all other "*watch*dog" efforts.

This "seeping-in" awareness to our minds, that thoughts do affect our daily life, can start to be the number one priority we start to process. We then will find there are some thoughts that if we do **not** invite to "sit a spell" or "wine and dine" them, the ideas will flow away from in-attention. Because of our developing wisdom, we will now be more selective and attend to the thoughts we do want to hang around. Now, that **is** being *watchful*!

I hope you now know that you are the *"watch*dog" of your thoughts. This awareness plants the *watch* seed in the "mind soil" of your brain to be fertilized and watered with constant vigilance of where your thinking is taking you. The crop you will harvest is the awakening attitude of how your thoughts affect your life in everything you do. And, that both negative and positive thinking is the fuel that feeds your whole being; mind, body, and spirit. It is up to you to be the *"watch*dog" over which thoughts you will allow into your mind to nourish you, and "set a spell!"

What do **You** think?

Chapter 24

XENOPHILIA

The "wonder" is in *all* people.
Do we not *all* bleed
the same color blood?

When we see a stranger, know that there is a "story" living inside that human form. In fact, there is a *great* novel residing within that person. If we do not take the time to open the "human cover" and listen to their experiences, we will miss the "story treasure" that resides within them. And, when an unknown person from another country, or even down the street, happens to have an accident and cut themselves, we should not be surprised to find the color of their blood is the same as ours!

There are seven billion human life stories on this planet! The awareness of this vast number of people in the world makes our life not less significant, but a wonderful addition. Think what we could learn from a neighbor of their culture, religion, family history, their way of dressing, and their dreams, fears, and hopes, if we would just talk to them! We might find we almost speak the same language when it comes to life aspirations or fears upon hearing about each other's personal lives and family. Maybe we are not such "strangers" after all!

The definition of *xenophilia* according to *Webster's* dictionary is, "attraction to or admiration of strangers or foreigners or of anything strange or foreign." Our attitudes, influenced by our thoughts, are intricately tied to our conditioned thinking, learned through our culture, family, religious beliefs, and infinite other ways, which affects our reactions to a stranger or foreigner. If we are lucky enough to have been taught, during our formative years, to be open to the excitement and wonder in all we see and meet, then we will view through a *xenophile's* eyes, which means we are open to or are attracted to and admire almost everything. This marvelous trait opens our mind to a library of priceless insight to the "people world" and to all of creation. What sympathy, compassion, and kindness for our global family could occur if we were receptive in our minds and hearts to other people!

There is a wonderful African greeting relating high praise to someone called *Ubuntu*, which translates roughly: "My humanity is caught up; is inextricably bound up, in yours." In other words, a person is a person through other persons. We do not have to go very far in this world to offer that salutation. It could be next door to us! *Ubuntu, to You!*

The opposite of *xenophilia*, is xenophobia, and the definition for the latter is, "fear or hatred of strangers or foreigners or anything strange or foreign," according to *Webster's* dictionary. Hatred is always rooted in fear, and fear is rooted in the unknown. However, if one does not know what the unknown is, how can one fear it? (I just added this for you to ponder, not answer now.) Our conditioned hate for the unknown is fueled through repeated stories of what transpired a long time ago, maybe even thousands of years ago. Sometimes we do not even know the why or the what, of the situation, we just hate! Of course, without some strong taught values of love for all creatures in our childhood, our xenophobia can be embraced later in life where we can encounter a variety of fear-inducing teachings.

Again, awareness is the key to how our fearful thinking about the strange or foreign absolutely affects our attitudes toward other people. It also helps to remember that we are the "unknown" in another country or down the street in our own neighborhood, or when we go to meet our fiancés family! Even unfamiliar clothing can offend or be viewed as "strange" in another country or in another part of the city, town, or village where we live.

As you can see, the concept of foreign or strange "is in the eye of the beholder." What we view as "really different," may be very familiar and not at all mysterious when seen by someone who understands what we are calling "strange." We can be filled with wonderment when we awaken to the fact, that it is our thinking, which labels something or someone as "strange."

Anger, war, fear and distrust are the result of our xenophobic thinking! However, awareness and information can give us insight to the "attraction" and "admiration" for the unfamiliar. Our view can change when we open our minds to listen and become aware of another's viewpoint, culture, etc.

With this thought in mind, I offer another meaningful greeting. This expression is the Indian Sanskrit word *Namaste,* which roughly translates, "I celebrate the place in you where we are both one." This greeting acknowledges that there are no ethnic, cultural, or religious invisible walls, just an inner knowing of oneness. It is this unique, mysterious, oneness of being; the sharing our life's journey on earth with other humans that we can celebrate. *Namaste, to You!*

Both the *Namaste* and *Ubuntu* greetings might be words and meanings you would like to write on your "blackboard exercise" notebook page to help memorize and embrace for your own heart. It may even help you see other people as your "world family."

What treasures lie within each of the worlds seven billion people! It is up to us to take the time to open the "human cover" to read, and understand each other's life stories, and to celebrate the beauty and richness of both our lives.

What would happen if we took the time and the effort to know each other?

What do **You** think?

Chapter 25

YOU

You are *You!*
Sooooo,
Believe in *Yourself!* Love *Yourself!*

Oh, the wonder of *You!*

There is no one else just like *you*. There is no one else identical to *you*. There is no one else who has the same DNA as *you*. Now, out of seven billion people in this known world, is this not amazing?

Oh, the miracle, the mystery of it all! It can give us goose bumps when we finally awaken to this phenomenon - that each one of us is unique!

When we discover how amazing each human being is, and can be, it then follows how important, and how critical it is to *believe in our self,* yes, to even, *love our self.* The scripture passage in Matthew 22:39 (NASB) states: "*You* Shall Love *Your* Neighbor As *Yourself.*" (Italics mine) I translate this passage as; "I have to love myself so I can know how to love another." For example, how does one teach another person how to play tennis if one does not know how to play or has played the game?

This way of "loving our self" is not a narcissist kind of love. It is not an excessive interest in our appearance or importance or

101

abilities. It is a belief in our self, as Rene Descartes seemed to confirm back in the early 1600's, "I think, therefore I am." He deduced that because he can think, he exists, therefore, he is! And, Aristotle said in the mid 300 BCE, "To be conscious that we are perceiving or thinking is to be conscious of our own existence." It is because we are alive, that we can start to value our existence and extend that thought to our care and consideration to believe and love our self.

We may now be starting to ask ourselves the silent questions: "How in the world do I start to; Believe in myself? Love myself? Know myself?" Here I propose the adage that may help us take responsibility for our own life. I wrote and used this in my 365 day devotional/journal book, *Lord, Today I Choose to Live Life's Adventure,* for January first: "My confidence comes from getting myself to where I want to go" and then I wrote "Today, I move my mind."

This is the deep secret: *Moving our mind will get us going.* Then, committing to this movement will keep us moving. "Remember, motion begets motion." Of course, we can always use some help along the way from other people or our reading different materials for our life's journey. However, it is ultimately up to us to decide and do that "whatever" we want to do, and this is also true in the decision - *to believe in our self – to love our self!*

The rediscovery of our self allows the "belief-seed" to sow itself in our mind, to germinate and grow, so we can harvest these traits: belief, trust, compassion, kindness, and love in and for our self. As I said, we have to know how to play tennis - to teach tennis! We have to know how to live – to truly live, life! We have to discover our self - to uncover our self!

By now, and with only one letter word essay to read, hopefully the title of this book, *Attitude 'Z' Reign A to Z,* has thread its way through all these writings and into *your* mind. Maybe *you* have become more aware and awakened to the impact and power that *your* attitude has on *your* life, from eye opening to closing, whatever 24-hour period of time that is, resulting in *your* behavior and actions. Remember, **you** are the "keeper of the key" into *your* mind where *you* will find a glistening treasure gift to unwrap and open: belief in and love of *yourself*. It is priceless! Protect it well!

The process of accepting and loving our self includes believing in our self, and this is a challenge we meet every day of our life! I have also encountered these with each essay I wrote. For remember, each word essay required delving into my mind for how to relate the word to our attitudes, which result in our behavior and actions. I needed to really believe in myself, trust myself, and love myself to ponder and write these essays. Doubts did seep into my mind and when that happened, I relied on one of "love's" definitions: "a strong liking for or interest in something," to help counter those thoughts. My interest was how our attitudes affect and determine our life, and this catapulted me into believing and loving myself enough to continue writing. It is not always easy to love and believe in myself in the things I do, but they are important to help me live a full rich life.

This is the twenty-fifth essay *you* have read. Hopefully, this will be the twenty-fifth trek to *your* "blackboard exercise" page where *you* now can write on "*You*." And the starting question can be: "Do you believe in *yourself* and love *yourself*?" This may be the first time *you* have actually confronted this type of question and tried to answer it. It may also help to write the affirmation from the beginning of this essay to seed into *your* mind: "Oh, the wonder of *You*! There is no one else just like *you*. There is no one else identical to *you*. There is no one else who has the same DNA as *you*…Is this not amazing?"

You, are *You!*
Sooooo,
Believe in *Yourself*! Love *Yourself*!

What do **You** think?

Chapter 26

ZONE

Our thoughts produce
our attitudes
that resides in our "Mind *Zone!*"

Well, we did it! I am writing the final alphabet letter, "Z" deciding on *Zone* for the word, and you are reading the final essay. However, you may have read this one first or anywhere in between the "A" through "Z" words. It does not matter for the process. And, I hope you have become aware that attitudes do not fit any chronological or alphabetical order. They intertwine themselves through all our encounters, behaviors, and actions. Attitudes are the results of our thinking forming our perception of all that we view.

As the heading for the essay on "Vision" states; "Everyone see's with a different *vision* than ours", and this book is all about helping us to become aware of how our attitudes determine our daily life by how **we** view things. This insight of how the "attitude thread" reigns in our mind will help us realize that any change we need to work on is preceded by our thoughts about it.

One definition of *Zone* according to *Webster's* dictionary is "Any area or *zone* considered separate or distinct from others because of its particular use." (Italics mine) We are definitely in a "separate or distinct" area, our mind or *zone*, when we develop and further our attitudes about everything. And, a further definition refers to *zone* as "a state that produces achievement in such extraordinary often unlikely, degree of success that it seems to defy purely rational explanation." Therefore, when we realize the importance our attitude is having in our life we now can weave this insight through all our thinking where being in the *zone* will "defy purely rational explanation."

Therefore, I am going to weave all twenty-five words into one long sentence beginning with *aware* and culminating in the twenty-sixth letter word *zone* to help reinforce the connection that our thinking, and interpretation for how we view life situations, affects our whole life journey. Thus, our "attitude thread" begins:

Being *Aware* is critical to knowing, and to be cognizant about something we first have to be awakened to it; then, of course, we have to know and be confident that our… *Belief* is our own, and that if a… *Change* in our life is needed, we can move through our… *Doubts* and be… *Encouraged* by building our confidence in the… *Fulfillment* of getting our selves to where we want to go; this knowing provides the thought seeds for our being… *Grateful,* that we have the power to fulfill our… *Happiness* from within; we also need to be… *Inclusive* and not label any… *Judgmental* thoughts about others or ourselves, using… *Kindness* as our thought driver through… *Life,* and knowing… *Movement* gives us energy to live in the… *Now* with a feeling of… *Oneness* with other people or things; trying not to always want or be … *Perfect* or to… *Quit* too soon: all this awareness can help us… *Release* our pent up fears, frustrations, anger, and other negative emotions, to be… *Soft* on ourselves and others, thereby using the absolute power of our… *Thoughts* to help us… *Understand* and to realize how we are evaluating life situations by using our… *Vision* to see with "new eyes" our need to… *Watch* our own thoughts and be alert that… *Xenophilia* is living in wonder and awe for admiring the strange and foreign; that to be… *You,* is to live your true actual self, which

106

puts you in your... *Zone*, because you are now aware that it is your attitudes that determine your behavior and actions and affect your whole life's journey.

The thought + attitude + behavior + action = knowledge is our enlightenment in giving ourselves absolute power to, "be able to be!" Therefore, the ultimate question, and one you might want to write on your "blackboard exercise" page for your last entry, is:

What Do **I** Think?

I now offer blessings and greetings from a few world religious and culture systems in addition to the two you have read in this book. The meanings are found in the Glossary in the back of the book.

Charis! Gakina indinawemaaganag! Shalom! Namaste! Ubuntu! Wai! Assalaamu Alaykum! to **ALL** creation.....

"Salute" from your fellow life traveler, Kathleen!

EPILOGUE

I think it took me seventy-nine years to know I believe in myself! I guess I always believed in me, but now I finally **know** I believe in me!

This awakening, this knowing, happened when I decided to publish this book. I now trust what I have written is worthy to be shared. This awareness does not curtail the fear in my thinking of "what if's," but belief in me, and what I have just accomplished through words is stronger, has more power, thus giving me confidence in myself through my own enlightenment. Trepidation is still there, but feeling empowered by this awareness in myself carries more weight!

After all this writing, I realized that a person's constant ruminant thinking, seeds "carry over" thoughts, and becomes an impossible burdensome load for the mind. Therefore, this idea inspired the following poem though my own awareness:

"CARRY OVERS"

With constant ruminating,
  doubting, stuffing, and query,
    "carry over" thoughts soon
      are an impossible load to carry.

When hurt by others
  in our vision's perceived thinking,

stay with it and deal with it,
    or have a lifetime of inner mind fighting.

Running, ignoring, and holding these thoughts
    drench wrinkled souls,
      and give us years on end
        for living in the doles.

These "carry over" thoughts
    are not good for the mind.
      They seed our attitudes,
        determine behavior and actions,
          harvesting a life that restrains and binds.

Therefore, watch all your "carry over's",
    both good and bad,
      to have a wonder – filled life
        and make your memories glad – not sad.

Wow! Writing, thinking, and pondering on how attitudes determine our day – our life, turned out very good for me. It is certainly a reminder to me of the affect my attitude has on **my** life journey. And, yes, from reviewing my own thoughts, I have a better attitude from the process of writing this book!

To be aware of where our thoughts are taking us is the key to enlightenment. May these words be a Blessing for Your Life!

What do **You** think!

GLOSSARY

Agape: A spontaneous, altruistic love, which is unselfish with concern for the welfare of others; selflessness.

Assalaamu Alaykum: Islamic greeting: May the peace and blessing of Allah (God) be with you.

Attitude Leaves: Words planted and rooted in our mind that can grow into our thoughts "leafing" out our attitudes.

Attitude Thread: Our attitudes, seeded by our thoughts, thread and weave through our whole being influencing everything we do.

Awakening Mind: Our enlightenment to something of which we have not previously been cognizant.

Awareness Seed: Insight, planted in our mind that helps us realize something for the first time or view it differently.

Beginning to Begin: Working through our perceived reason not to start, so we can begin.

Belief Seed: We plant this idea in our mind to rediscover and believe in our self.

Beliefs Thinking Dungeon: Beliefs, buried deep in our mind conditioned through our ancestors, culture, and religious structure.

111

Blackboard Exercises: Pages in the back of the book where we can write our thoughts, ideas, and concerns for reflection and consideration.

Charis: Christian greeting: Grace, which affords joy, loving-kindness; a favor freely done without claim or expectation of a return. Unconditional love.

Cotton Ball Soft: A sensory touch image, reminding us to think softer, kinder thoughts when we encounter people, things, and events.

Dark Grey Gloom: A metaphor for the coloring of our attitude proceeded by our thinking

Dark Mind Cave: Thoughts that lay deep in our mind until we become aware to acknowledge them.

Doubt Thread: A doubting thought that weaves itself through our minds, entangling through our attitudes, and keeping us from living life to the fullest.

Dungeon of Dark Thoughts: We are engrossed in our own dark mind thoughts.

Eye of the Beholder: All things available to be seen are viewed through our own eyes.

Full-Fill-Ment: "Full:" I am all together; "Fill:" I can continue to fill myself up to live a satisfied life for myself; "Ment:" I am meant to be here, so I can do what I need to do.

Gakina indinawemaaganag: Ojibwe expression: Reflects a belief that there is an underlying connection and oneness through all forms of life: people, animals, birds, insects, trees and plants, and even rocks, mountains, and valleys.

Giver: A person believing they are responsible for someone else's happiness.

Golden Glow Beam: An invisible radiance emitting from our presence, reflecting to everything around us.

Habitual Thinking: Programmed thinking reinforced and conditioned through family, culture, religious training etc.

Human Cover: Another person's life story which stays hidden unless someone is willing to open up, hear, and listen, that they each might share similar joys and sorrows.

Inner Need: Something that is deep in our mind that wants to be acknowledged and recognized.

Insight Awareness Treasure: Insight gained through taking the time to talk to not only friends and family, but also people we do not know.

Keeper of the Key: We hold the key for believing in ourselves. No one else!

Keyhole Opening: Small awareness insight to our mind.

Keyhole Thought Vision: Insight awareness into our mind about something we have not acknowledged before.

Kindness Habit Seed: A thought planted within our mind where we nurture gentleness and kindness to people and things.

Light Bulb Awareness: To become aware in our mind of something that we have not recognized or acknowledged before.

Locked In Perception Thinking: A mind that defines, labels and identifies people, ethnic groups, religion or belief systems into a one-way thinking.

Loving Kindness Eyes: It is an Agape kind of love, which is unconditional, benevolent and intentional toward all things and precedes kindness.

Mind Prisons: The place where our thoughts reside that can limit or freeze our attitudes.

Mind's Eye: Inner seeing that we consciously may not yet be aware.

Mind Zone: A distinct area, our mind, where we develop and further our attitudes about everything.

Memory Gift: Any adage or phrase we write down and memorize to help our attitude in life situations.

Mental Garment: A thought we slip on which covers our attitude about things.

Mind Baggage: Any thoughts we pack in our mind and carry through our day and possibly our whole life.

Mind's Door: An insight waiting to be recognized.

Mind Fabric: Our thoughts cover all we perceive as our reality.

Mind Questions: Questions we have from habitual conditioned thinking or current events in our life.

Mind Sea: Thoughts both negative and positive; going 20,000 leagues deep in the depth of our mind.

Mind Soil: Thought seeds planted in our brain to be fertilized by awareness and watered by constant vigilance of where our thinking is taking us.

Movement Begets Energy: Motion stimulates energy for our mind, body, and spirit.

Namaste: Old Indic Sanskrit greeting: I celebrate the place in you where we are both one.

Needer: A person, who believes other people are responsible for his/her happiness in life.

New Perfect: Something we call "perfect" can change because of a new scene, new awareness, or a new thing we add: we then can have a New Perfect.

Now Power: We only live in the present moment and that is where we accomplish things.

Old Landscapes: Seeing something we have looked at many times with a new viewpoint.

Oneness Seed Thought: Developing an attitude for recognizing our oneness in all human beings; that we can have unity in spirit, even though different, and diversified, in our thinking.

Only Way Thinking: A person believing that their way, their beliefs, their idea is the way everyone else should believe, follow, and live.

Perfection Burr: Trying to be or have something perfect. A thought entangled in our mind that things have to be perfect.

Push/Pull Feeling: Our inner dialogue debating of: to do or not do? to go or not to go? thinking.

Seed Thoughts: Ideas planted in our mind.

Separateness Seed: Alienation of co-workers, different religious groups, ethnic groups, neighbors and any other possibilities in the universe when we identify, label, or define them with absolute judgment thinking.

Shalom: Jewish greeting: wholeness, wellness, and serenity

Soft Print: An imprint we can leave through our awareness of how we affect society.

The Crazies: Sharp, imaging thoughts, that pierce into the mind and bleed a rough day through our behavior.

Thinking to Yield: Becoming aware that we can relax, surrender, or let go of something that may be controlling and hampering our life.

Thought Thread: A thought that weaves through our mind, affecting our thinking, attitude, and behavior.

Ubuntu: African greeting: My humanity is caught up, is inextricably bound up, in yours.

Wai: Buddhist greeting: Well being, mutual recognition (graceful gesture of greeting)

Watch Dog: A person that watches over their thoughts to protect them from the effect of negative thinking.

Wonder Filled: A state when we are freed from the influence of negative thoughts and can view the world with new eyes and enjoy life fully.

Word Seeds: Any words that we seed into our mind which will grow and sprout through our thoughts, blossoming into our attitude harvest.

ACKNOWLEDGEMENTS

Where to begin! I have come to realize that writing the first draft of my book is the easiest part. It is what comes next; the rewrites! and rewrites! and rewrites! that sometimes consume and overwhelm me. Thus, it has become apparent to me, that my sanity is kept intact by all the help and support I receive along the way on this venture and is absolutely priceless.

As I said in my previous book, *Lord, Today I Choose To Live Life's Adventure* acknowledgements: "No [woman] is an island entire of itself; every [woman] is a piece of the continent, a part of the main" by John Donne in the 17th century. This statement means to me, that there is nothing we do to survive in the world that is not helped, in part, by someone other than ourselves. We truly are an interdependent species! However, we often try to do all things, all by our self. But for me, I believe, with the vast number of people in this world and the variety of their gifts, it behooves me to make myself available of them.

The following people have been a blessing, and literally a mind saver to me in helping keep my attitude on an even keel. I used the power of my thought, to know and accept that I do not have to do this adventure all alone. And, that I can avail myself of their expertise and support to help keep my attitude in check. I also refer to the quote from Proverbs 15:22 [NASB] frequently to remind me of this:

Without consultation, plans are frustrated.
But with many counselors they succeed.

119

The blessing of a supportive spouse is priceless, and Dick has been this, unconditionally. It must not by easy for him to be around a partner who is silent, staring into space with an "in the room physically but mind elsewhere" presence as I have been doing while working on this book. This has been a two and a half year, on again-off again, writing process, so his patience is monumental, and "nary has a harsh word been spoken" or has judgment of any kind made about me. To unfetter someone is to free from restraint of any kind, and this behavior of his has been liberating for me.

Another support for me, and, an invaluable one, is a writer's group I belong to where I do not have to censor my work or my emotions, therefore making me feel free to express myself. These three people: Carol Peterson, Lynn Pagliarini, and Dave Fabio, each with their unique gifts & talents, have been a supportive environment for me. Carol has read, reread my essays and put the little voice "watch your quote signs and Italics" in my mind as I write. She has had a challenging job! Thank you, Carol!

Lynn also has read, reread, and editing along the way, she asked questions that made me think, rethink and then, think even deeper to help flush out what I was really trying to say. I finally, started mentally to use the words "clarify" and "clarity" whenever I began to broach her margin notes. Thank you Lynn, for your gift of "clarifying!"

When a writer uses a computer, they should have a "live-in" technician to keep that blasted machine operating. Especially if one is as borderline computer illiterate as I am. Dave almost fulfilled that in residence job by being just a phone call away. He kept my computer operating when mysterious things happened, and of which, I had no clue, what! For me, insanity and computers are bedfellows and my sanity only stayed in check because of Dave. Thank you seems trite, Dave, but it comes from my heart. So thank you all, for helping keep me working, and functioning! Because of these three people supporting me, and I keeping my thoughts in check, there is a book, and I truly **do** know "Attitude'Z' Reign A to Z."

One other group, which I have been a part of for over twenty years, is my Thursday morning "Cluster of Women:" Bea Jackel, De Larson, Dee Nelson, Georgeane Karnuth, Marlene Harty, Pat Hoyt, Ruth Hedlof, and Sandy Kotval. They all bring a variety of ideas, talents, philosophy, life styles, and political and religious views to these weekly sessions. But, the unifying threads that weave through all of us is trust, respect, acceptance, and love for each other. Now, of course, we do not agree about everything! We are human beings, you know, with different backgrounds, up bringing, and belief systems. However, the interest, caring, and concern we have for each other is our universal bond, and it is what drives us to "show up" each week. Believe me; being connected with such a "gathering" can help keep one's attitude in check or at least from sinking into really deep "doo-doo!" I recommend you to take advantage of such a group if you have the opportunity, or, why not start one yourself?

Yes, we are not an "island entire of itself" for it takes an infinite number of people to make something happen. In addition, this is certainly true in the example of writing this book. Moreover, it is not only all these people in my life who have given and done so much for me while working on this book, but as I write with this pen, on this paper for example, I think about how many people it takes to make just these two products I use, make all this writing happen. So thank you, thank you, thank you, to all you unknown! You, and what you do, are also invaluable!

Family, friends, even strangers makeup a gigantean force that can help a person accomplish something. Recognizing and using our awareness for when all this help can be useful, is and can be an awakening in our mind. For me, it strengthens and ever refreshes me to, "Keep On Keeping On." Help along the way can make our life's journey lighter, and it certainly did this for me on my writing venture.

Peace and Thank You

Kathleen....

BIBLEOGRAPY

Campbell, Joseph. *A Joseph Campbell Companion.* Selected & Ed. by Diane K. Osbon New York, NY: HarperCollins Publishers, 1991

Dalai Lama.H.H. *The Policy of Kindness.* Compiled & Ed. By Sidney Piburn Ithaca, NY: Snow Lion Publications, 1993

De Mello, Anthony S.J. *Awareness.* New York, NY: An Image Book, Published by Double Day, 1992

Deng Ming – Dao. *365 Tao Daily Meditations.* New York, NY: HarperCollins Publishers, 1992

Dyer, Dr. Wayne W. *Change Your Thoughts, Change Your Life.* Carlsbad, CA: Hay House, Inc. 2007
_____. *Excuses Begone!* Carlsbad, CA: Hay House, Inc. 2009

Frankl, Viktor E. *Man's Search For Meaning.* New York, NY: Washington Square Press, division of Simon & Schuster 1984

Funk, Margaret Mary O.S.B. *Thoughts Matter.* New York, NY: The Continuum Publishing Co. revised 2005

Luhrsen, Kathleen M. *Lord, Today I Choose To Live Life's Adventure.* Enumclaw, WA: WinePress Publishing 2001

Nepo, Mark. *The Book Of Awakening.* San Francisco, CA: Conari Press 2000

New American Standard Bible. The Foundation Press Publications. Box 277, La Habra, CA: The Lockman Foundation. 1971

Peale, Norman Vincent. *How To Have A Good Day Every Day.* Pawling, NY: Guideposts Outreach Publication 1961, 1981

Ruiz, Miguel Angel MD. *The Four Agreements.* San Rafail, CA: Amber-Allen Publishing Inc. 1997

Shaklee Sr., Forrest C. *Thoughtmanship 10 Rules For Happiness and Contentment.* Pleasanton, CA: Published by the Shaklee Corporation 2004

Templeton, John Marks. *Discovering the Laws of Life.* New York, NY: The Continuum Publishing Co. 1994

Sweeney, Michail S. *Brain The Complete Mind.* Washington, DC: National Geographic. 2009

Tolle, Eckhart. *The Power of Now.* Novato, CA: New World Library 1999: Originally published in Canada by Namaste Publishing Inc., 1997
____. *Stillness Speaks.* Novato, CA: New World Library & Vancouver, Canada: Namaste Publishing 2003

Webster's New World College Dictionary Fourth Edition. 2002. Willey Publishing, Inc. Cleveland, Ohio

BLACKBOARD EXERCISE PAGE

BLACKBOARD EXERCISE PAGE

BLACKBOARD EXERCISE PAGE

BLACKBOARD EXERCISE PAGE

BLACKBOARD EXERCISE PAGE

BLACKBOARD EXERCISE PAGE

BLACKBOARD EXERCISE PAGE

BLACKBOARD EXERCISE PAGE

BLACKBOARD EXERCISE PAGE

BLACKBOARD EXERCISE PAGE

BLACKBOARD EXERCISE PAGE

BLACKBOARD EXERCISE PAGE

BLACKBOARD EXERCISE PAGE

BLACKBOARD EXERCISE PAGE

BLACKBOARD EXERCISE PAGE

BLACKBOARD EXERCISE PAGE

BLACKBOARD EXERCISE PAGE

BLACKBOARD EXERCISE PAGE

BLACKBOARD EXERCISE PAGE

BLACKBOARD EXERCISE PAGE

BLACKBOARD EXERCISE PAGE

BLACKBOARD EXERCISE PAGE

BLACKBOARD EXERCISE PAGE

BLACKBOARD EXERCISE PAGE

BLACKBOARD EXERCISE PAGE

BLACKBOARD EXERCISE PAGE

Kathleen Luhrsen is an author, wife, mother, grandmother and a great-grandmother. She worked as a Parish Visitor in Evangelism and Outreach, and Coordinator of Older Adult Ministries for Trinity Lutheran Church in Stillwater, Minnesota for twenty-six years.

She is the author of <u>Lord, Today I Choose To Live Life's Adventure</u>. It is a 365-day, three year, Devotional/Journal. She and her husband live in Minnesota.

.

CPSIA information can be obtained at www.ICGtesting.com
Printed in the USA
BVOW071326230613

324021BV00001B/12/P